PRAISE FOR LONG-LOST MOM

Yolande Essiembre's Long-Lost Mom *is a powerful and courageous exploration of trauma and resilience. Following the decades-long journey of one mother's reunification with the son she gave up for adoption forty-six years ago, it's a memoir that speaks to the healing power of reconciling with ourselves and with our pasts. Essiembre skillfully and directly addresses how the secrecy of governments and church-run institutions affected a generation of women who were shamed into giving up their children for adoption. A deeply compassionate and wholly engrossing story. I cannot recommend it highly enough.*
- Trevor Corkum, author

As a former director of a non-profit agency working with single parents for over three decades, I appreciated reading and highly recommend this book. Long-Lost Mom *is an intimate story about the author placing her child for adoption at birth and reuniting with him forty-six years later. Anyone having experienced fear, shame, love, loss, and reconnection will be able to relate to her struggles, strengths, and difficult decisions along her journey. Sharing her story is a remarkable act of courage and generosity.*
- Nancy J. Hartling, ONB

What a powerful, painful, inspiring and moving story that will touch your heart and give many people hope and help. Long-Lost Mom *is beautifully written, a book you will not want to put down until it is over.*
- Ruth Fishel, author of such titles as Time for Joy, Wrinkles Don't Hurt, and The Joy of Aging Mindfully

I'm honoured to write this endorsement for Long-Lost Mom *by Yolande Essiembre. Her story gave me the opportunity to see firsthand that the women I worked with, and advocated for, for many years, can survive and thrive. This book is about surviving trauma while living with guilt and fear for many years. It is also about the opportunity, forty-six years later, to continue on her healing journey. It is an incredible and true story of overcoming and becoming who she is today: a successful, strong, kind, and loving woman, friend, and mother.*
- Pamela Warner, Wisconsin USA, former outreach worker for Tri-County Council on Domestic Violence/Sexual Assault

In 1990, a friend in the United Kingdom traced the woman she believed to be her birth mother and asked me if I would make the first contact. It was a profound experience when I met with the man who, from the resemblance, was clearly her brother. When he invited my friend to meet with their mom, I knew she had found the family she had yearned for all her life. Yolande Essiembre has written a book from the other end of the relationship—the mother's experience of being discovered by the child given up at birth. Long-Lost Mom *is a moving, revelatory story shared mostly in silence by millions of families. It will help the mothers who hold the secret of the hole in their hearts; it will help the children, now adults, whose lives have been fragmented by being separated at birth and who wonder what it would be like to reunite.*
- Warren Redman, author, and founder of the Emotional Fitness Institute

If you want a book you can't put down, then Yolande Essiembre's Long-Lost Mom *is for you. Not only is it a gripping read, but it's the true story of a young, unmarried mother's reunion with the child she gave up for adoption years before. It is a heartbreaking story that reminds us of how we have shamed such women and the untold damage such negativity creates in the lives touched by it. But it's also heartwarming that mother and child experience the miracle of reunion and that healing of old wounds is always possible.*
- **Susan Amos, author, playwright, and columnist**

Long-Lost Mom *is a captivating story of reuniting with a child who had been place for adoption 46 years prior. Through her storytelling, Yolande allows us to bare witness to intimate moments shared between her and her son – from the first emails exchanged between them, to traveling to the other side of the planet to meet him in person. This book is sure to pull at your heartstrings and give you hope for your own reconciliations.*
- **Mary Morrissey, Founder of the Brave Thinking Institute**

LONG-LOST Mom

MY JOURNEY OUT OF HIDING

YOLANDE ESSIEMBRE

Long-Lost Mom
Copyright © 2022 by Yolande Essiembre

Tellwell Talent
www.tellwell.ca

ISBN
978-0-2288-7025-8 (Paperback)
978-0-2288-7026-5 (eBook)

TABLE OF CONTENTS

To my son Trevor:
May you always remember that, in my heart,
I never forgot you.

PREFACE

E veryone has a story. Events in our lives, the paths we choose, the beliefs we hold on to, and the people who surround us are all part of it. Why is our story so important? The part of my journey that I chose to share in this book is about hiding from such a large part of my story that I was essentially hiding from myself. As an unwed mother in the '60s who gave up a baby for adoption, I spent most of my life hiding my guilt, shame and, yes, even my pain. When my son found me forty-six years later and gave me the chance to make another choice, I did. I was afraid, and I had few answers and many questions: How would I tell my three other children? How would I face the truth buried in my heart and in my mind? How would the life I had built be changed? Slowly, as I unravelled my past and embraced the whole story, I became free. It is possible to heal, and this is what I want to share by writing this book.

Several months after my son found me, I discovered I was not alone in my experience. Ours was part of a greater story. In Canada, historical data from Statistics Canada (1999) reveals that almost six hundred thousand infants were born to unmarried mothers and were recorded as illegitimate births between 1945 and 1971. Because of social, cultural, and religious beliefs of the time, most unwed mothers were pressured to put their children up for adoption, especially those who were in homes for unwed mothers. This practice was also common in the United States, Australia, New Zealand, and the United Kingdom. Adoption records were sealed, which meant very little information was revealed to the adoptive parents, and no information was available to the adoptees or to the biological parents. I was one of these unwed mothers, and my son was one of these babies.

As I write, thousands of adoptees and biological parents are searching for one another. In Canada, the United States, and other countries the laws on obtaining information about an adoption are changing and information is becoming more widely available. Some welcome this openness while others are worried about the implications this will have in their personal lives. My intention in sharing our story is to bring a ray of hope and understanding to those living similar experiences or to those supporting them. It is a story about hope; about overcoming shame and self doubt; about healing and making peace with the past.

CHAPTER 1

I Am Found

In the post office of the small town where I live, on the coast of New Brunswick, my heart pounded and the blood drained from my legs. I held the small envelope in my hands and knew immediately what it was about. A few days after returning from a trip to Japan—on May 31, 2016, to be exact—I picked up my mail. Having been away for the past three weeks, my mailbox was full. At the counter, I sorted out the travel magazines and discarded the flyers from the grocery store and the hardware store. Amongst the envelopes I decided to keep, a Canada Post card advised me to pick up an item at the service counter.

"Good morning, bonjour. We have a registered letter for you this morning," the clerk announced in her usual friendly manner.

"Really? I can't imagine what it could be."

The brown envelope led me to believe it was a business letter. Probably a copy of my tax return or something about my pension. It was the return address which stopped me in my tracks: *Department of Social Development, Fredericton, New Brunswick.* I stood motionless over the envelope on the counter. My heart was racing as I slowly opened it and realized it was from a social worker. My mind sped back in time to 1970, and a high-pitched screaming seemed to fill my ears. I knew my life was about to change. I needed to sit down to read it through. Adrenaline pumping through my body, unsure of my steps, I slowly made my way to the car.

Dear Mrs. Essiembre,

I am writing to you today because I am trying to locate Yolande Frenette, who resided in Saint John, New Brunswick, in 1970. I believe this person to be you.

Please be kind enough to contact me to discuss an important personal matter.

Oh my God! He is looking for me! I immediately knew what this was about but I wanted to remain in denial and not admit it to myself. I knew I would have to make the call to the social worker. But before doing anything, I needed to take care of myself. My heart was beating so fast and my ears humming so loudly that I was worried about my blood pressure. I drove home in a stupor, taking the back roads.

The post office in Shediac is on one of the streets leading to the water. To local residents, this is known as the old part of town. When I was young, Shediac was very small, consisting of one long main street with most of the population living in homes built on or between Main Street and the Shediac Bay. I remember the day we moved to Shediac. My father had been appointed manager of the grocery section of a large general store built by Mr. Tait, a wealthy and well-respected man who lived with his family in a mansion on Main Street. It was said that he owned half the town of Shediac. I was five years old at the time. We arrived by train—a big, beautiful steam engine as black as the coal that kept it moving. My dad took me by the hand as we walked down Weldon Street to Bay View Court. The court was also known as the Horseshoe because the ten houses were built in a semicircle. They were called war time houses, built to create jobs after the war. Our house in town was new; it had an indoor toilet, taps, running water, and a bathtub! The house my parents had been renting before had only an outhouse, and inside there was a pump on the kitchen counter to draw water. I didn't know how our furniture had arrived but the rooms were already furnished. My mom and my older brother were there waiting for us on that cold, sunny December day in 1951.

Knowing I was in no shape to drive, I took these old, familiar roads. Leaving the post office, I drove down Calder Street, turned onto Shore Drive then up Weldon Street. I passed Bay View Court and the small house where my dad died five years after we had moved in. Generally, I always notice the house, but on this day, lost in a haze, I couldn't manage it. I do not even remember driving down the street where I live. The next thing I knew I was already at home. Standing at the front door, I fumbled with the key. Nothing seemed to fit anymore!

In the safety of my home, I fell onto the sofa and re-read the letter: "an important personal matter," it had said. I sat for a long while, conscious of every breath, feeling uncertain that the next breath would be a given. Gazing out my front window at the green grass and leaves shimmering in the breeze, I latched on to anything that had a hint of movement, trying to draw in life energy. I felt so weak. As my past caught up to me, time seemed to stand still. I knew I couldn't refuse him. It would be so awful to be rejected twice by the same mother. I knew I would have to meet him, if that was what he was asking. I was scared but also, if I am honest, relieved at the same time. Finally, the worrying would be over. My secret would be out. No more fear about how or when I will tell my other children. No more worrying about what would happen if I died and they had to deal with this alone. I felt overwhelmed, submerged, tossed about by the current of emotions that threatened to sweep me away, and yet I could also feel, somewhere inside, there was a courageous knowledge that I could survive. I had been through worse. I knew I needed to calm down before taking any action. Forty-eight hours, I had learned, is what it takes for your body and mind to regain stability after receiving a shock. I would make the call in a few days when I would be ready.

In the meantime, I would strive to keep my everyday life as normal as possible. Long ago when things would go wrong and I felt down, I learned that if I made someone else happy it helped me cope. I first learned this lesson when my husband and I separated. When I found myself feeling sad or discouraged, I would visit a friend or family member—someone I knew was often alone—rather than stay home with my thoughts. Sometimes I would talk about my sorrows, other times I would listen as they spoke about their own. It helped me to understand that I was not alone with my troubles and difficulties. Other times, we would simply converse about happier topics, and for a few hours we would forget our woes and worries. Regardless of how we spent our time together, I always left feeling a little stronger and more at peace.

In this way, I resolved to take the time I needed to digest this information. In the meantime, I had friends to visit and I would get back to my regular activities of yoga, Pilates and pickleball as soon as I could. Tomorrow, the sun would rise and I would have breakfast and tea as usual. The world would not stop even if I was distressed. I would tell no one yet about my news, this information that threatened to upend and reorder my life. I did not need other people's opinions or fears to add to my own. This was my journey. I needed to move forward at my own pace—by myself and for myself.

CHAPTER 2

Seeking Balance

Day One

The next morning when I woke up, I lay motionless. I kept my eyes closed longer than usual. I slowly opened one eyelid just a slit. The room was still painted blue. Sunlight was streaming through the space below the blind. I needed that little glimpse of reality. I closed my eyes again. A thought filtered through my mind. *Was this a dream or had I really received that letter?* I listened to my heartbeat and focused on my breath. *Breathe: inhale, exhale,* I repeated as I coaxed myself out of bed.

I went through the motions of my regular routine. My morning meditation was short because I was caught up in thought, only occasionally connecting with my breath and repeating my mantra. After my regular yoga practice, I hurried back to the comfort of my sofa. I just wanted to be alone. I did not want to speak to anyone. I tried again to quiet my mind, but there was too much turmoil for it to settle. The same question rolled around in my mind: *What am I going to do? What am I going to do, but what am I going to do?* To distract myself, I reached for my iPad. I had a message from Hay House in memory of the self-help and spiritual growth author Dr. Wayne Dyer. He spoke of making every situation positive. How could I possibly make this situation a positive one? It was the situation I had feared the most for forty-six years! Dyer's words at least offered my mind the possibility of a new direction. One final tip captured my attention: *You can choose not to be emotionally immobilized.*

As I pondered Dyer's words, I felt a glimmer of hope. It had been twenty-four hours and I was not dead yet! I decided to carry this thought with me throughout my day. I peeled myself from the sofa and visited a sick relative who I knew was waiting to hear about my trip to Japan.

I got through the day.

Day Two

Life had been good the last few years. My children Paul, Danielle and Natalie, were adults, with their own lives and adventures to live. Even though two of them lived in other cities, I felt close to each of them. Today's technology and the possibilities for easy travel make the bonds easier to maintain, but I always looked forward to our in-person visits.

My mom, who had lived with me for almost six years, had recently passed away. For three years, I had been retired and I enjoyed a lot of freedom. It's true I found the first six months of retirement challenging. I worked in Human Resources, mostly in wellness and conflict management, for fifteen years. I had loved my work and the people I worked alongside, and it was a fulfilling. job that allowed me to be of service, use my creativity, share my knowledge, and feel valued. I chose to retire because the policies and direction of the department were no longer in line with my beliefs and values. Immediately after retirement, I found myself feeling without purpose. I felt I had done it all: children, marriage, divorce, education, career, and travel, all in that order!

But now what?

Once retired, what was I supposed to do with the rest of my life? I did not want to do something simply to fill in the emptiness of my days. I wanted to continue to grow emotionally and spiritually.

It was around this time that I discovered meditation. I had seen an ad about a weekend session—Introduction to Meditation— which would be presented close to home, so I asked my youngest daughter, Natalie, if she was interested in going with me. Although personal and spiritual growth were not new to me, when I learned about the benefits of meditation, it opened up a whole new world. I had strived to become happier and healthier for many years, and I was privileged to share what I had learned with others through my work. Meditation was another way of achieving this; it had become another tool in my toolbox. And now, with the letter from the Department of Social Development arriving in the mailbox out of the blue, I needed meditation more than ever.

The clock was ticking; forty-eight hours had passed since I received the letter from the social worker. The tightness around my heart was constant, and although I knew I must make the call, I didn't feel ready yet, so I decided to give myself another day. I knew the call would be about the son I had given up for adoption. I feared the news; I did not know what to say or what to do. I knew that underneath the story of his adoption lay a much deeper story. One which, in my shame, I had struggled to tell anyone, and which I had not yet reconciled. So how could I begin to tell my children? How could I tell anyone? How could anyone ever forgive me for giving up a baby? How could anyone understand why I hadn't spoken about it for so long?

I could tell that if I continued in this line of thinking, it was going to be another long and agonizing day. I needed to find inspiration somewhere, so I listened to an online meditation which spoke about the energy of attraction and saying we have the power to manifest our desires.

But what was my desire? What did I really want?

I could not change the past nor could I change what was happening now. What is, is, and what was, was! That morning I was inspired to keep my attention on my desire rather than focus on what I did not want. I reached for a writing pad and formulated an intention before it escaped me. I wrote: "My intention is that this adventure I am about to embark on will be positive for me, for my children, and for everyone involved. My intention is to focus on the truth." This was my desire. I did not know what the future would hold or how the journey would unfold. All I knew for certain was that the social worker had news.

CHAPTER 3

The Time Had Come

Day Three

The sleeves on the T-shirt were too long, the pants too tight, and black would be too warm for today. I was indecisive as I prepared for Pilates class. It was Friday morning, and the big decision had to be made. Any other decision was an annoyance. I even debated breakfast: cottage cheese or yogurt? Toast or bagel? Every ordinary choice was impossible. I knew I had to make the call and reach the social worker before the weekend. My mind was made up: This had to be done before leaving for Pilates. Mornings are usually when I have more energy and feel strongest, so I knew if I delayed the call any longer I might back out. Pacing the length of my condo I reached for the landline, took a deep breath, and dialed the number.

A man answered and introduced himself as I sat on the sofa. He sounded friendly yet professional. In the letter I had received, he was direct and to the point. I barely gave him time to say his name before I stated my case.

"My name is Yolande. I received a letter from you this week asking that I call you about an important matter. You have the right person. I know why you're trying to reach me. I did have a son in 1970, and I gave him up," I said all in one breath.

With a kind voice, he interrupted my confession.

"I understand this must have been a difficult call for you to make. I want you to know that you do not have to give any information if you do not want." There was a short silence. "You must have been shocked to receive that letter."

"Yes, I couldn't call you right away because I needed time to calm down. I was afraid I might have a heart attack. It is all quite overwhelming."

"It must be," he replied. "However, I needed to inform you that your son has filed a request to get some information about his biological mother and to find you if possible."

My heart was thumping so loudly I could almost hear it. I inhaled and then exhaled slowly, but I felt a churning fear in the pit of my stomach. Using a technique I had learned in meditation to calm myself down, I inhaled again—a long, deep breath—and then exhaled through pursed lips, as though blowing through a straw. Thoughts were flashing through my mind, and I could not grab a single one to reason it out and make sense of it. Forty-six years of holding back had suspended my fears in time. I had struggled to organize, heal, understand, forgive, and forget over the years while avoiding the emotions I ultimately knew I had to face and deal with. This was the moment when everything exploded into reality. I was talking about my past, about giving up my son, on the phone with an actual social worker.

How far would I open that door? Could I open up to the past where I kept my words, thoughts, and my body's own language under lock and key? Locked inside, they remained untouchable so I did not have to feel them again. If I set these thoughts and fears free, would they invade my world again? Would they choose a path of their own, like flowing water that carves rivers and paths over land? Opening up would be to risk losing control. The social worker's voice brought me back to the present moment.

"I must remind you that all the information about the adoption remains confidential and the files are sealed. I cannot reveal any of it without your consent. I could send you a consent form, if and when you want it. I have permission to give you information about your son if you would like to hear it."

I agreed.

"Your son wants you to know that he is well. He would like some information on his birth family and knowledge of his bloodline. Sounds like he has some medical questions. He wants you to know that the adoption went well. He now lives in Vietnam, and he is the director and manager of a second language training centre and runs a small restaurant. He said he had a good mom who died in a car accident after he finished high school. His adoptive father and maternal grandmother are still alive."

I did not even flinch at the news that he was in another country. Vietnam was so far away, like something out of an unbelievable tale, similar to the unbelievable experience I was living. It was comforting to know that he seemed to be doing well, and I was sorry to hear the news of his mom. I asked no questions, keeping the information at bay as much as possible, trying to integrate this new reality into my ordinary life.

"Would you be open to communicating with him or providing some information to him through me? We often recommend not going too fast in giving your identity and information. I could send you the consent form, and you can let me know exactly what information you are willing to give to him."

I kept silent for what seemed a long while, but he respected this silence.

"I really don't know."

Holding back tears, I remembered one of the mornings I did not want to recall. That awful morning where I had to pronounce the final words that would make it all legal. There could be no turning back. The words were stuck in my throat today in the same way as they had been on that terrible morning so long ago. At last, I was able to compose myself enough to speak.

"One thing that is clear to me is that I would never have searched for him," I said.

Forty-six years ago, I stood with a social worker in front of a judge and answered his questions. Following the social worker's declaration stating that I was placing the baby for adoption, the judge asked: "Do you relinquish all rights and responsibilities for this child?" In the stillness of the courtroom, I uttered a weak "Yes." Had I not heard that "Yes" echoing, I would not have believed I said it. It did not feel like it had come from me, yet it had. On that day, my twenty-three-year-old mind understood that I was never to look for him nor try to contact him.

But something else was clear. I knew that if my son ever found me, I would not reject him. I had always feared he may show up on my doorstep someday, but I could not even let myself imagine the scenario. Now it was happening. Sure, he was not on my doorstep, but he was searching for me. I could at least answer his questions and give him the information he was seeking. However, I didn't think I could meet him because I did not know how I would react.

"Does he know I was raped?" I asked the social worker.

After hesitating, he said he would check the file. When he returned, his voice resonated in my ear.

"No, there is nothing in the file that indicates he has been told," he said.

I took a deep breath and searched my heart. Could I do this? Could I let my son into my life? *What is, is,* I repeated to myself. I gave birth to this child. I carried him inside my body. He is part of me. There is no denying it, even if I had tried to escape this reality for forty-six years. Words tumbled out of my mouth as I explained to the social worker the reasons I was so afraid to be in touch with my son.

"First, how do you tell a person that his biological father is a man who raped you?" I asked. "I just cannot see myself saying that."

At the end of the line, the silence told me that the social worker understood. I could feel a trembling in my belly, as if the presence of that baby were still in my womb.

"I may be able to help you," the social worker finally said. "I am in touch with him. I could tell him myself if you give me permission. He needs to know the truth."

I gave my permission.

"The second reason is that I am afraid to see him, physically. I have gone to counselling for many years and have worked through the pain and the shame of that event. Still, as I speak about it right now, I feel fear in my body. What if he looks like his father? I have no conscious memory of what that man looked like, but I know that the image is registered somewhere in me. I am afraid of my reaction. What if I faint or slam the door in his face? I cannot even imagine standing in front of him. I do not want my son to be hurt again by my reaction because he is in no way responsible for what happened."

There was another long pause.

"Do you think it might help if you saw a photo of your son?" the social worker asked.

I thought about it for a few moments.

"Yes, that might help," I said. "I feel I would be ready now to at least look at a photo."

I gave permission to the social worker to contact my son to let him know that I had been found and to share the details of our conversation. I was still shaken when I left for Pilates, but I knew doing exercise and taking care of my body was healthier than retreating to my sofa and worrying, so I made the effort.

CHAPTER 4

First Letters

I turned the page of my calendar; it was already the first weekend in June. I stepped outside onto my patio to enjoy the warmth of the sun. The air was fresh with the scent of the tall pine trees in the backyard. A pheasant, parading her nine baby chicks, quickly made a turn to the back of the house when she spotted me standing there.

"Don't run away," I whispered as they picked up speed and ran off. "Don't run away, don't run away…"

I was deep in thought, already running away from that beautiful moment. I was replaying the conversation with the social worker in my mind, thinking about the news I had received the previous day. I did not know when I would hear back from him or get more news, but I anticipated the weekend would be long. Part of me was trying to figure out how to navigate my new reality. The other part of me wanted to participate in life just as it presented itself on a daily basis. *Are you going to stand here and mull over what you have no power to change today?*

The choice was evident. June had arrived. It was time to plant flowers. The annual ritual of choosing flowers was one of my favourite spring outings with Natalie, and today we would visit the nursery to choose our favourite plants. After making our choices, we would plant her flower beds and make several lovely arrangements to adorn my patio and front door entrance. At the nursery, the pansies smiled at us, the daisies looked so proud and the impatiens encouraged me to be patient. I was in awe as each variety spoke to us in its own language. As we prepared the soil for new growth back at the house, there was a deep knowing that life energies would take care of growing the seedlings. I was reminded that so it would be for me. If I took time to prepare the soil of my heart, new life would grow from the seeds of hope that I had planted there. It was a happy day. I was content spending time with Natalie even if, at times, I felt uncomfortable not sharing my secret. But I was not yet ready to talk about it.

The bubbling energy of my great-niece and great-nephew was contagious and kept me entertained on Sunday as I visited with my sister and her family. Sunday dinners were a tradition in our family, and while my mother had been alive we were almost always expected to show up. It gave her great joy to prepare a meal for us and top it off with one of her famous lemon pies. My sister had carried on the tradition with her children and grandchildren. I would join them sometimes, mostly on special occasions, but I appreciated the invitation on this particular Sunday. Once again, I remained silent about what was happening in my life. I wondered how much my sister, who is six years younger than I, knew about my past. It was so long ago and she would have been so young when I was forced to make my choices. I had no memories of us discussing the situations I had gotten into after leaving home. Regardless, this Sunday would not have been an appropriate time for a discussion. Besides, my priority was to tell my children first. I would deal with family and friends later on.

As I opened my eyes Monday morning, I gave thanks for a new day even if I was worried about what would happen next. After yoga, I routinely sit in one of the white leather rocking chairs in my living room. I usually choose the one facing the window so I can admire the old pine and maple trees growing just beyond the fence in my backyard. I watch the squirrels and chipmunks run at full speed along that fence, and I keep the screen door open so I can hear the birds chirping while checking my emails. That Monday morning, it occurred to me that I was sitting on the sofa again. It had been my place of refuge for the past week. Perhaps I needed something more massive and solid to sit on. Perhaps it was because there was so much motion inside me that I could not rock; I needed to feel grounded. Regardless of the reason, I found myself on the sofa as I quickly scrolled through my inbox. Even though I was hoping to receive news, I was taken aback when I noticed an email from the social worker.

> *Dear Mrs. Essiembre,*
>
> *Included are two emails I have received this morning from your biological son. As you will see he will not be sending you photos, and you will understand why as you read his email.*
>
> *If you are still interested in pursuing a contact with your son, please let me know so I can facilitate this for you. If, for whatever reason, you decide not to continue this path, please advise me so I can in return advise your biological son.*

I had not anticipated hearing from my son this soon! I felt light-headed and shaky. I was scared yet could not wait to read his message.

The first letter from my son arrived on June 8, 2016.

> *Memories... This was not my intention in trying to find my birth mother, and I am truly sorry for what has happened. I understand a lot more now, and I do not want her to have to tell her children about me because she thinks they have the right to know. They do not need to know about me. Maybe it is too late and maybe I should have replied sooner on this*

regard. Tears came to my eyes when I read that I had other family members.

She should not feel remorse… She should be proud that she gave me a chance in life.

A note from the social worker was included, indicating that I had requested some recent and older photos to help break the ice.

As a child growing up it was not easy having ginger hair (a carrot top) and freckles. I was discriminated against in many ways and fought a lot. It made me very strong, and I would not change a thing now. I am one of those who became better looking as I grew older. I do not believe sending pictures at this time would be wise on my part, as I do not want to be judged again on my possible resemblance to my birth father. If anything, it should be she who sends me pictures of my bloodline and family. I think if my birth mother truly wants to know me… she can communicate with me directly through email at this address. She can create a fake account and I will never know who she is. In time I will send all the pictures she wants, but she must first know me. Know who I am first.

Again, I will say that her children do not need to know anything at this point in time. I am not here to gain anything other than the truth and knowledge of my bloodline. I am not here to cause problems. I have very little of a family now. I am very close to my (adoptive) father, but that is it. My family is truly the one I create. They can be a part of it if they choose.

I hold nothing against her. I somehow knew everything you told me before I got this email. Nothing surprised me.

Trevor

I put my iPad down on the sofa and had to take a few breaths to let every word sink in before moving on to the second letter.

The simple truth... I am not sure if she will want to continue communication with me or not. I only want truth and honesty. I do not lie regardless of the outcome. I wake up every morning with an attitude that I can make my life better and for all those who work for me. Together we make plans and work together. I know my purpose in life and it is to help people. That is what I do every day.

I said I had a good adoption, and that is not a lie. I was taken good care of. Although, after my mother's death I was on my own in many ways and I made many mistakes in life. I have, in many cases, learnt the hard way. I have been to hell and back several times, and I grow from these experiences. They make me stronger and wiser. I never live in the past. I learn from it. I hope we can find a bridge of communication where the past will not get in the way. :)

You can quote anything I have said here to my birth mother. I do believe she should understand me better before continuing any communications.

Stunned and unable to react, I sat with tablet in hand staring out the window. I struggled to grasp the reality that this was my son writing to me.

My mind travelled from past to present trying to make sense of it all. The image that came to mind was the one and only time I had seen him. I had caught a glimpse of a tiny baby being wheeled out of the delivery room on that morning he was born, and it was like having my heart pulled out of my chest. I closed my eyes and cried while they wheeled the bassinet out of the room.

"I love you. Goodbye. God, please take care of him," I said silently.

I brought myself back to the present and slowly re-read the letter. Suddenly, I began to laugh as I realized what he had said. *Red hair, he has red hair!* I was so sorry to hear that he had been bullied at school—but oh my God—I was so happy to hear my son had red hair. That meant that he probably looked like my family. My father, whom I loved so very much, died when I was ten years old. He had red hair. I felt the fear and the tension slowly seeping out of my body. A little flicker of joy and hope lit in my heart. *Red hair*, I kept repeating over and over in my mind, *I love red hair!*

I wrote to the social worker, thanking him for sending me these letters and asking him to send me Trevor's address. He had mentioned in the letter that I could write to him directly, but the address was not included. The social worker explained that he had censored the letter and was obliged to take out any identifying information until both of us signed the consent forms, which he would be sending to me. Until then, if I chose to write to Trevor, I could send the letter to him and he would make sure that Trevor received it. In the following days, I signed the consent forms. I created a non-identifying email address as Trevor had suggested, and I sent in the information to the social worker.

The wharf in Shediac where I spent my childhood days happens to be only a few minutes' walk from my home. During summertime as a child, my friends and I would walk there almost daily. It was our hangout spot, a happy and carefree place where our laughter and squeals echoed all the way up the street. We spent hours sitting there and talking about our hopes, dreams, and worries while watching the tourists being rafted to their yachts anchored in the channel.

It was where I had learned to swim. It was there, in the days after receiving my son's letters, where I went to ponder and reflect upon how one might answer such a personal letter. I was learning to swim in the profound waters of relationships, emotions, and fears. I had re-read the letters several times, letting his words flow into my heart like a refreshing stream washing away the hurt, soothing the path, clearing the debris. I was comforted by his words.

She should not feel remorse... she should be proud that she gave me a chance in life.

It had never occurred to me that I could be proud of giving him a chance in life because I felt so much guilt over not keeping him. I had felt so much shame—the shame carried by "unwed mothers" of the time.

After a few days, I simply let my heart dictate the following email to my son.

June 15, 2016

Trevor, thank you for your message. I am happy to know your name. And I am glad that you wrote me. The social worker forwarded your emails to me but was not able to give me your email address. He was out of the office for a few days so that is why it took so long for me to answer. He has informed me (and probably you) that we both need to sign a consent form to give him permission to exchange our emails. I agree that we should communicate directly as it could save a lot of misinterpretation. I will get in touch with him to sign whatever I need so that we can exchange emails.

I would like you to know that you are not causing me trouble by seeking me out. On the contrary, as difficult as it may seem, I think it is a gift. We have a lot to learn from each other.

I honour your courage, and I also want to live in truth. It may not be easy to untangle all the knots, but I believe it is an opportunity for us to grow. When I received the letter from the social worker, it was a shock even though I knew all these years that it could happen. I knew immediately that I would not reject your request and that I would contact him. But I needed to give myself time to integrate this new information and calm down. I was shaken up and felt a rush of adrenaline and a flood of memories going through me. It was a roller coaster of emotions, some fears and some worries, some joy and happiness but mostly a great sense of relief. I am happy to have the opportunity to communicate with you. After a few days, I felt calm and was able to call the social worker.

I will be telling my three other children about you not because I have to, but because I want to. I have wanted to tell them for a long, long time but I didn't know how and didn't know when it would happen. I needed to be OK about it within myself before being able to speak with them. Now I know I can tell them, and I feel good about it. I will be visiting my son at the end of June, so I will speak to him first. I will be talking with my two girls shortly after that. Believe me, it is a great gift for me to be able to do that. It has weighed on my heart for so many years. The four of you will decide after that if you wish to communicate and form relationships. They, like you, are strong and are truth seekers; I love them very much.

Trevor, I think you were right in not wanting to send me photos at this time. I do want you to know that I was not the one who asked for photos right away. When I spoke with the social worker, I was relieved to get news about you. I am so happy that you are alive and well, that you had good parents and that you wanted to know about me. But my biggest fear was that you would ask about your biological father and how would I tell you. I asked if you knew that I was raped. He said he could tell you. I knew getting in touch with you also meant getting in touch with the past and, as you probably know, events are registered in our bodies. Sometimes when I talk about it, which is very rarely, I still feel shaky inside.

I mentioned to the social worker that one of my greatest fears was that if I ever met you, I really didn't know how I would react. I was afraid that you would feel some rejection by my reaction whatever it may be. It was then that he asked if getting a photo might help. In wanting a photo, I was trying to protect both of us—you from feeling a rejection and me from facing the harsh reality of the rape. I have healed a lot over the years and, with your contact, I now know that I still have some healing to do. That is OK. I will take care of it. It is clear for me now that in my mind there are two stories: one about the baby I gave up and one about the rape. They are separate. Something about that leaves me feeling peaceful. I am no longer afraid to judge you again "on your possible resemblance to your birth father." I thank you for your honesty. You are like an open book. Believe it or not, people often said that about me. Little did they know that I had a big secret!

Anyhow, it made me smile when I read your email because you mentioned having red hair. My sister and I have always shared the desire to have a red-haired child because our dad (your grandfather) had red hair, and we loved him so much. He died when we were very young. My sister won. She had a beautiful little girl with red hair. I love her dearly.

Trevor, I do want to get to know you. Thank you for giving me that chance. Even if we are strangers to one another, I did give birth to you. You are my son, and by reading your email, I recognize that we are alike in many ways. You are a forty-six-year-old man, and I am a sixty-nine-year-old woman. Both of us are very strong and most of all want the truth. That will be our bridge for communication. I am sorry for all the pain I have caused you, but I am happy that I was able to give you a chance in life.

Thank you for writing,
Yolande

I waited anxiously for his next letter, wondering if I would ever hear from him again. It took several days for the social worker to gather the required documents and get the consent forms approved. I remained silent about what was going on in the meantime and tried to work things out within myself.

When I encountered people I knew, I did my best to act normal, smiling and chatting about my wonderful trip to Japan. While describing the beauty of Tokyo, Kyoto, and Osaka, I talked about their amazing castles and temples. Not to mention the thrill of riding the bullet train at 320 km/h between these cities. I recalled the serenity of the Japanese Alps, the hot springs and the shrines. Occasionally, when the conversation was longer, I spoke of the devastation of the atomic bomb still depicted and solemnly remembered in Hiroshima. Or I would tell one of my favourite stories about being lost in the city of Kamakura. After visiting the Great Buddha, we were given time to go shopping. Stepping out of a candy shop, I was distracted by a street vendor and lost sight of my friend who had continued to walk amongst the crowd. Unable to find any members of our group and not knowing the language, I wandered aimlessly for about an hour not recognizing any of the street names. Fearing the bus would leave without me, I was about to lose hope and begin to cry when I heard a voice call my name: "Yolande! Where were you? Never mind, just run!" We were the last passengers to board the bus. I was grateful to have a recent and exciting subject to hide behind.

The chatter in my head was constant. Even if I tried to meditate, the chatter was louder than the mantras. There were very few moments of peace. The boat had been rocked. In recent years, I had managed to sail along smoothly for the most part, having submerged all the events of the past deep in my subconscious. Now I had to deal with the waves of memories that kept flooding my mind. Dwelling in the past brought back feelings of sadness, shame, and guilt, and when my mind darted into the future, I felt anxious. I did my best to refrain from creating stories that would frighten me, but doubt started to creep in. The voice in my head was broadcasting many warnings: *You do not know this man! What are you doing? You are sixty-nine years old. This man is forty-six! Should you be sharing your personal information?*

The social worker had said not to go too fast and advised me to tread carefully before divulging too much. I knew nothing about this person. If I took away the words "my son," I had no idea who he was. Once again, I was confronted with two stories. In the past, there was the story of a son to whom I had given birth. In the future there was a stranger who wanted to know something about me. That was very scary. All I could do was try to stay anchored in the present, observe my thoughts, and do my best not to get caught up in them. I repeated: *Today, I am okay. Today, I am safe. Today, all I know is that I have a son who is looking for me.*

Then one day, the letter arrived.

June 21, 2016

Hello Yolande,

Wow! It is absolutely fantastic that I have found you. I have always wondered about you, and I have always wanted to meet you. I, too, believe it could be a gift, and I will admit that I am not sure where to begin… I think if it were my child meeting his birth mother for the first time after all this time and he asked me what he should do, I would tell him or her to begin from the beginning.

My shoulders dropped, and I breathed easier as I read these words. I smiled, and my hand covered my mouth as if to stop myself from speaking. My heart was happy, but my initial feeling was that I didn't have the right to be happy about this. Because of the shame, my past was like an anchor still holding me down.

In his letter, Trevor told me that he was adopted in early infancy and spoke of his parents. He talked about his childhood and where he was brought up. He had spent most of his summers at the beach, jumping off high bridges, and running in the forest.

My parents broke up when I was about six, and I did get into a lot of trouble at that point. I was very rebellious, I was a wild kid and, even then, I had no fear. I was very athletic, played every sport, climbed every tree, and always went where I wasn't supposed to go. I can tell you from my birth until I went to school, I was a happy, energetic young boy.

He also told me of the businesses he is managing in Vietnam, an English language learning center and a small restaurant. He apologised for not writing sooner.

I was so happy to write back!

Hi Trevor,

I was happy to read an email from you once again. It all seems unreal to be able to write to you. I have often talked to you in my mind but never wrote to you. I'm sorry that I only gave you access to a little bit of information. I thought that you had a good idea to create a new email address for now. Thank you for allowing me time to adjust. For now, I am comfortable with that. It keeps our correspondence separate and is more private for me.

Once my other three children know about you, and once I feel more comfortable about all this, I will give you more. I am happy that you have found me and happy that we can write. Don't worry about only writing when you can, I understand that you have a busy schedule.

I will be looking forward to your next email.

Yolande

CHAPTER 5

From Silence to Guidance

It had been almost a month since I received the social worker's letter. Some days I felt overjoyed, relieved, and excited about the news. Other days I was scared. I had not yet found the courage to tell anyone what was going on, not even my best friends. Silence over a secret is like a roof over your head. It protects you from the rain of judgements, the downpour of shame, the thunder of accusations, and the uncertainty of the unknown. Stepping out from this safety made me feel very vulnerable. The thought of being exposed, of not knowing how the truth would be received and how my life might be changed, kept me immobilised. It was safer to remain silent than to speak out, yet it was becoming increasingly difficult living under the pretense that nothing was going on. It was difficult not talking about my life as it was or sharing my sadness and joys with the ones I loved.

Truth is a powerful life energy. Like the flower concealed in a bud, it wants to bloom. In order for truth to flourish, the bud has to crack open; it has to cease being a bud and take on a new life. I was about to crack open! I needed help, another pair of ears to hear my confusion, another heart to hold my broken one. It was time for me to move from silence to guidance.

Rachelle, who has a calmness about her that is inviting, came to mind. She had been a schoolteacher, and having found the public education system very stressful, she chose to leave her teaching career to follow a lifelong passion in wellness and personal development. With an interest in nutrition, she decided to explore and add non-traditional healing methods into her repertoire. Rachelle remains an educator, offering advice on nutrition and teaching yoga and other wellness practices in our community. Most important to me is that she is non-judgemental and open, as well as being my yoga teacher. Before I knew it, I had picked up the phone.

"Rachelle, do you have some time to spare? I need to speak to someone about something that is going on in my life, and I think I need help."

"I am free right now if you want to come over. I will see you in the yoga studio."

On the drive to Rachelle's house, I argued with myself. *Maybe I don't need to talk to anyone. I'm doing just fine. What am I so afraid of?* As I stopped at a red light I contemplated turning back. *I'll just go and have a chat with Rachelle. I could just ask her a few things and then leave. What am I so afraid of?*

The yoga studio is a lovely sun porch attached to her home where I come several times a week for yoga practice. It is usually one of my favourite places to relax, meditate and connect with my inner self. Today it was causing me stress. Rachelle greeted me at the door, and I glanced at her silently.

"Come sit down and tell me what is happening," she said.

In spite of my great desire to remain silent, we had no sooner sat on the sofa when I blurted out: "I need to tell someone. I have a second son. He lives in Vietnam. He's forty-six years old. I can't believe he is alive, and I can't even believe he is for real. He is looking for me. He found me!"

I didn't want to cry, but the tears spilled down my face. They were old tears, ancient tears that had been locked in my heart for so long. Tears of sadness from giving birth and not having a baby to hold. Tears of shame. Tears of helplessness and tears of grief for who I was and all I had gone through. I knew this was an occasion to heal. The choice was mine. I could allow myself to feel the pain and learn to become more compassionate towards myself or I could hang on to my hurt. I could choose to swallow it up again. I did not want to continue living from a place of fear. I wanted to be free, and the road to freedom was to unlock the secrets of the past, face my fears, and let them go. It was time to step out of my cage. Trevor had given me the key by reaching out to me. Now it was up to me to open the door and step out. Not an easy thing to do. Rachelle was silent but very present.

"Tell me about your fears," she said, handing me a tissue.

"Some of my fears sound so unreasonable it is silly to express them. I feel they are almost like monsters. They dwell and thrive in the dark. They want to remain hidden, unidentified. This week while trying to figure things out by myself, out of curiosity I looked up the definition of monster in the dictionary. It said it is: 'An imaginary creature that is typically large, ugly, and frightening.' My fears are the same. I find it difficult to voice them out loud, to put words on them, to acknowledge and admit that I have them."

"We both know," she reminded me, "that the only way to make fear shrink is to shed light on it. What is your worst fear?"

"I am worried about how all this will affect my children. I have heard stories about how adult children would sometimes turn against their parents because they had not been told of a family secret. So, I am afraid to reveal my secret to my children because of this."

"Do you believe deep down within yourself that your children, as you know them, would turn against you?"

I took a moment to go within and think of my three children. I could feel the love welling up in my heart: the love I felt for them, and the love I felt coming from them.

"No, in my heart I do not truly believe this. I know they love me. They are kind and loving and would not turn against me."

It was the stories in my head, the constructed fears, which were keeping me prisoner.

"What else are you afraid of?"

"That it will all go wrong!"

She asked me what *it* was and how it could *all* go wrong.

"A long time ago, I attended a session on personal growth," I said. "One woman shared that she had found her son after twenty-eight years, he came to live with her family, and she was very happy. I was touched by her story, knowing it resembled mine. A few years later, I heard through another person that things did not go well at all for them. The husband had become jealous and left, as had her other children. I never confirmed if this was true. I did not know this woman personally and never saw her again to ask if things had gotten better. I just assumed that the lesson to be learned was that it could all go wrong."

Talking about this helped me understand that I had adopted this belief many years ago when I was married and had young children. I must have thought that remembering her story would keep me safe and prevent me from making the same mistake. I had carried this belief until the day I met with Rachelle, when I finally began to question its validity. It was now a belief that no longer served me, and it was time to let it go. Rachelle agreed.

"Some fears," I shared, "are disguised as slight worries. The kind of worries that create a constant nagging in my subconscious. Like a shadow lurking in the background, warning me not to go there and especially not wanting to be named. I get a glimpse of it and then it disappears. One of these fears came from something I learned in a psychology class on group dynamics. Whenever there is a shift in one person in the family, it will often have an effect on the other individuals. I worry about how this would affect our family dynamics."

I was afraid that bringing someone new into the family would be difficult. How would it affect Paul, Danielle and Natalie? When the children were young and I came home with a new baby, I prepared them for the new arrival. I had a favourite story that I shared about how a mother's heart is not like a pie; it cannot be divided or run out of pieces. A mother's heart and love grow with every new addition, and no one person can replace the other. My children were no longer small. They all were adults, including the new forty-six-year-old I might introduce to them. Nonetheless, I worried about each of them and how my decisions would impact their lives.

"You have no power over this," Rachelle said. "You cannot control or change how your children will feel or react."

She helped me understand that I could only support them as best I could in the situation, so I decided to continue to grow my life and trust that my children were strong enough to deal with the truth. I reminded myself of the intention I had written out a few days after learning my son was searching for me: I wanted to focus on the truth, and that this would be a positive experience for me and for all involved.

Still, I had major fears about meeting my son. Who might he turn out to be? He could be a drug dealer or not a nice man who might be difficult to form a relationship with. I was afraid that because he lived in a communist country that it might not be safe to be in touch with him. These and other worries frequented my mind.

A few days before leaving to visit my oldest son, Paul, and his family, I decided to share some of my fears with Trevor because I felt I was being distant.

June 27, 2016

Hi Trevor,

I'm writing to you because something is troubling me. I am happy you have found me, and I would like to get to know you. I hope someday that I will be able to meet you, but I am a little worried and if I want to be honest with you, I must admit that something is holding me back. You say you have no fears and I believe you, but I do. I do not want to put myself or anyone else in danger. I just want to know that you are really safe and that there is no danger for you and others who are close to you.

I also have a question: Is it okay if I share all this information with your brother and sisters when I speak with them about you? Or would you rather tell them about your life yourself? I want to be honest with all of you, but you also have the right to create your own relationships and share your own stories and your life as you see fit.

Hope you are well.

Yolande

CHAPTER 6

Revealing the Secret

I visit Paul and his family, who live quite a distance from me, every year. That year, I had booked my flight sometime before finding out that Trevor was seeking me. I had no idea how I would tell my eldest son that he had a brother who was fourteen months younger, but I knew I would tell him during this trip. Even though we live thousands of kilometres apart, when we get together it is always as if no distance exists between us.

The first two days of my visit were packed with activities. The four of us—my daughter-in-law, my youngest granddaughter, Paul and I—decided to spend our first day together at the park. It was a perfect day. The trees were dressed in the soft green leaves of spring and freshly blooming flowers perfumed the air. We sat beside the lake, marvelling at the pink and white water lilies. We revelled in ice cream treats while catching up. I wanted to hear all about what was new with their work, what they had been up to since my last visit, and what their plans were for the coming summer.

After dinner, I was happy to talk about my trip to Japan, to show photos, and offer a few gifts. The aqua silk kimono and the kokeshi Japanese doll delighted my granddaughter whom I still lovingly called "little one" even though she was ten years old. On every one of my visits, she and I spend hours in the gazebo talking, laughing, reading, writing, doing art, playing card games, and simply enjoying each other's presence. We typically walk to the playground and indulge in "make believe time" during which she invents a game and Grandma has to learn and follow the rules.

We also play pickleball, fly kites, and swing on the monkey bars. This trip would be no different; nothing would interfere with the pleasure of each other's company. As a result of the full day, I had little time to think about the secret I was planning to reveal, and the next day was just as busy. The weather was perfect, and the in-laws came over for a barbecue, so it was a great excuse to avoid the subject I was so afraid to broach.

To my surprise, the conversation happened spontaneously on the third day. Paul and I were alone. We had just finished breakfast and were enjoying tea and coffee while making plans for the day. Perhaps we would take a long walk in the park or visit a museum. Somehow, discussing the possibility of visiting a museum brought up the subject of old stories and history. Paul revealed that his wife had a growing interest in genealogy and someday might look into researching her family history. That triggered everything for me, and I spoke before I could even think about how I was feeling.

"By the way, talking about family history, I have something to tell you." I knew I had his full attention. "Do you remember a long time ago when you were in college, I told you I had been raped when I was young? What I didn't tell you was that I had a baby. I couldn't keep him. I had to give him up for adoption. I was afraid I would never be able to love him because of what had happened. For many years I simply could not talk about it. How could anyone forgive me for giving up a baby?"

"Oh, Mom! That is huge! I'm so sorry to hear that happened to you," he said.

Silence filled the kitchen while Paul did his best to recover from the shocking news. I was lost for words.

"It was a very long time ago. I had to give him up."

He wrapped his arms around me and held me for a moment. Then, very slowly, he got up to pour himself more coffee and offer me another cup of tea. As he processed what I had said, his body language gradually changed.

"What are you saying, Mom? Are you telling me I have a brother?"

He seemed quite happy to hear there was another male in the family. He had a brother. Wow! My husband left the family when Paul was twelve years old, so he had grown up with me and his two sisters. Eager to find out more about his brother, Paul pressed on with questions.

"Have you ever met him? How old is he? Where does he live?"

I explained that, coincidently, Trevor was brought up in a village close to the small community where the four of us moved after being separated from my husband.

"I have never seen him. I don't know what he looks like. He told me that he has red hair and that he attended a French school."

It was when I mentioned Trevor's last name that Paul almost fell off his chair.

"I think I know him, Mom! He was on the same school bus and came to our school!"

His eyes travelled from left to right, from past to present, as he connected the dots in his mind. His hand rose to cover his mouth. It was as if he couldn't bring himself to say aloud what he had just discovered.

"F…! Mom, I know him! He was teasing some younger children on the playground and I told him to stop. When he didn't stop, I jumped him and we got into a fight. We were brought to the principal's office! I sometimes tell that story and remember it so well because it was the last physical fight I had when I was in school."

My heart skipped a beat. I sat quietly in disbelief. How could this be? Why had I not figured this out? I had never thought of the school bus, and it never occurred to me that the children from the two communities attended the same school. But it all made sense now. In one of his letters, Trevor told me he had been a very happy child until he was six years old and started attending school. His first year had been a very difficult one. His parents separated, and he was picked on and made fun of at school because of his red hair and freckles. He had been so bullied that he became a bully who often got in trouble and into fights. It was now my turn to be in shock. My little red-haired son had grown up almost right in front of my eyes for many years. Every time I watched Paul play soccer, enjoy a baseball game, participate in track and field or attend a school activity, Trevor was also playing. Both were in the same sports! He was there in front of my eyes all those years, and I didn't know.

"What do you say we go for a walk, Mom? I think we could both use some exercise and fresh air. There's a park not far from here."

We crossed the busy highway, both of us putting the morning conversation on hold. We walked mostly in silence through a wealthy neighbourhood, noticing the large, beautiful houses with impeccably manicured landscaping. When we entered the intimacy of the park trails our conversation also grew more intimate.

"I can't believe all you went through, Mom. You were so young. It's hard to understand."

"It is difficult for me to explain how things were back then. In today's world we can hardly imagine how it was in those days."

Memories began to project through my mind like an old slide show flickering across a screen. Choppy sentences, snapshots of events, all separate in a way yet all related in my past. I did my best to paint a picture of how I remembered it. In the small, mostly Catholic town where I grew up, the culture was very much influenced by the Church and its rules. Women and girls did not have much say in decision-making, and they were expected to be good, to be obedient and modest and at the service of others. Rules about sexuality were dictated by the Church as well. One clear rule was there would be no sex before marriage, and the unspoken rule was that the females were expected to be the guardians of this code. We were expected to know better, to keep a man in his place and to not let him have his way. Sex was regarded as unholy, shameful, or even dirty, and was only sanctified after marriage for procreation. In many Catholic families, sex became an obligation after marriage no matter how many children were born. The word "sex" was not spoken in public. There was always something secretive about it. As a result of this taboo, there was an innocence and ignorance among teenagers and young adults. Birth control was practically unheard of and was not approved by the Church. There were many myths about how not to get pregnant, and sex education did not exist. Sex was spoken about only in secret, in dirty magazines and in books which were kept hidden under the mattress and considered to be risqué. It was like the elephant under the rug; it was there but no one publicly acknowledged it.

I had been given a kitten once, and I named it Sex. I don't know why. I suppose it was to affirm my independence since I was now grown up, living in a different city, and working. In those days, we were considered minors until the age of twenty-one even if we lived independently away from home and were working. Shortly after receiving the kitten, I had to move to a new apartment building where pets were not allowed, so I took the kitten to the SPCA and asked that they find a good home for it. The person in charge refused to accept it because of its unacceptable name.

When sex was mentioned, the language was not one of respect and mutual responsibility. Men "scored" while women "got caught." Men had sex and were proud of it and were encouraged to boast about it. Girls "slept around" and were "trash" if they did and "Miss Goody-Two-Shoes" if they didn't. There was great shame brought onto girls who became pregnant while unmarried. These young women were labelled "unwed mothers." They would often be sent away and be in hiding until their "illegitimate child" was born. Most of these girls were considered unfit to take care of their child, so the babies were taken from them and put up for adoption. Once the pregnancy was over, they were expected to go on with their lives as if nothing ever happened. Psychology had not yet understood there were after-effects. Often, women were thought to be too emotional, hysterical, too sensitive and weak. Men knew best; they were strong and rational. They were the leaders of the Church, governments, and communities.

I grew up in this culture of the late '60s and felt the peer pressure of becoming modern, becoming open to making my own decisions about my life and about sexuality. The extent of making my own decisions had been to name a kitten Sex. I had no intentions of having sex with anyone, much less of sleeping around. I attended a private school for girls which I loved and graduated from in 1965. When asked what I wanted to do in my life, my response during my teenage years was that I wanted to become a flight attendant (they were called stewardesses at the time), but I had secretly carried a dream since my first year in school. I had seen a presentation about poverty in Africa and about the orphan children who were being cared for in orphanages. I wanted to become a missionary nun, go to Africa, and care for orphan children. I told no one about this except my close family. I loved children and said I would never have any of my own because there were already too many children in the world without parents. Once I graduated, I even entered a convent for six months, but I soon learned that community life was not for me and there were no guarantees I would ever get to Africa. If I took a vow of obedience, the choice would not be mine to make, so I had to return home and replan my life.

My first experience in love ended sadly. I was broken-hearted when my first love ended our relationship after his first semester at university. As much as I wanted to register at university the same year he was beginning, I had not been able to because of finances. As a result, I decided to work for a few years. We visited on weekends, but after he did poorly that semester, his parents forced him to drop the girlfriend.

My second long-term relationship was with a kind, loving, and respectful young man in his last year at university who loved me more than I loved him. I left him after meeting the father of my first son. He reminded me of my first love, and I was very drawn to him. After a few months, I became pregnant.

I was scared when I learned I was pregnant because I knew my whole life was about to change. A feeling of powerlessness and defeat swept over me. I felt helpless, similar to someone falling off a cliff. Inside me, I could hear an echo of a loud "Nooooooo!" There was something familiar about that feeling because I experienced it when I was ten years old and my dad died. Until then I had been an ordinary ten-year-old girl, and life unfolded in an ordinary manner. The morning of his death, my external life changed and I was forced to look internally for answers. There were none. Everything my life and security had been built on was gone. I lost my dad, my home, my friends, my school, and my community because we had to move away. In a way, I felt I also lost my mom because she was no longer the same after that morning. Even God, in whom I had been taught to put all my confidence in, was not who they told me he was; he could not perform a miracle and give me my dad back.

Nothing was the same. People did not look at me in the same way. I was no longer just Yolande; I became the poor little girl who had lost her father. My presence brought on feelings of sadness, of loss, of pain. Sometimes this would be expressed by people looking at me through teary eyes, and other times they simply looked away. Others gave me gifts perhaps to make up for the loss and soothe my pain. Still others offered privileges such as being excused for not having done my homework or pushing another child on the playground.

"After all, it wasn't her fault," I would hear, "her dad just died."

I even sensed an unease and discomfort with my friends. If we didn't want to talk about the death of my father, we seemed to be without words. I searched inside me for the ordinary little girl, but

I could no longer find her. I had a new identity; I was an orphan. A label had been thrown upon me for everyone to see. A tornado had swept away my ordinary life.

Learning that I was pregnant at twenty-one brought back that feeling of powerlessness, and I noticed many similarities. Again, the way people looked at me changed. This time, I felt the look of reprimand, judgement, disappointment, and, occasionally, sympathy. There was no tornado this time. It felt more like skidding on an icy road, losing control and being unable to put on the brakes. The way I looked at myself changed as well. I was once more taking on a new identity, and I would wear the new label "unwed mother." Again, I withdrew within and watched the life I knew fade away. I lost the respect of others and respect for myself. I lost my dreams, my future. I was not proud of myself. I spent many hours alone in my room crying and listening over and over again to "Sounds of Silence" by Simon and Garfunkel. There was a familiarity about this, like being in a bad dream unable to awaken. Who I thought I was, was no longer. I was now one of "them," one of those girls who were judged and looked badly upon because of the shame. I had brought it upon myself.

I broke the news to my boyfriend through devastated, broken-hearted, frightened tears that flowed uncontrollably, but he offered little support except to come with me to tell my mother. Once there, we lacked the courage to tell her, and my brother was the one who broke the news after we were gone. We went to see a priest and asked to be married. He met us together, then interviewed us separately, and then together again in what seemed to be less than an hour. The final conclusion was that he could not perform the ceremony because this was not a marriage made in heaven. Evidently, my boyfriend was not ready for marriage and only wanted to marry me because I was pregnant.

Because of the beliefs of society at that time, pregnancy before wedlock brought shame onto our families. My mother had recently been remarried after ten years of being a widow. She was marrying a good man, the father of four sons. My younger sister was still at home, and I knew my mom's heart was broken when she told me she was in no position to help me. My boyfriend's parents wanted him to return to university and threatened to withdraw all support if he didn't. His mother met with me to let me know they would arrange for me to go to a home for unwed mothers and would pay the expenses, but I refused. There was no way I would hear of it. After getting over the shock of being pregnant, I became attached to the little life growing inside me. I had no idea how I would manage, but I was determined to keep my baby. The man whom I thought would be by my side for life left, and I was alone with my pregnancy.

I did consider myself to be more fortunate than many other young girls who were younger or still in school. Many would be sent away against their will and have their babies taken from them. I was twenty-one, legal age, so I could make my own decisions. Before this happened, I was living away from home and had a wonderful job working in a hospital with children who were mentally challenged or had a physical disability. I loved my job and the children whom I cared for in the previous two years. When I became pregnant, I was asked to resign because I was pregnant and not married. I did not even see the injustice in this because I was immersed in this culture of judgement and blame; I was grateful for the opportunity to resign as opposed to being fired.

"It could be seen badly on a resumé," one of my superiors said. "Once this is over, you can move on with your life."

My three girlfriends and I had to let go of our apartment because I could no longer pay my share of the rent. I was "homeless," but that term was not common back then.

The need to care for myself and my unborn child was stronger than being approved of at the time, so I filed a paternity suit and, because I had no money, a law student defended my case. My boyfriend's parents came to court well-prepared with a good lawyer and hoping to prove their son was not the father. I will never forget that morning in court when my boyfriend left his parents' bench, stood in front of the judge, and declared, "I am the father." I knew what that meant for him. The case was closed, and his courage fuelled mine. His honesty touched me deeply and helped restore some of my dignity. They lost more than a court case that day. They lost a grandchild, my boyfriend lost a son, and my future son lost a father.

I found a job as a live-in nanny and worked there until my son was born. Looking after the couple's baby boy gave me some joy and a place to live. On weekends, I would crash at a dear friend's apartment. She and her husband had a beautiful baby girl whom I adored and who gave me hope. And so I got through the next few months living partly in fear and sadness and partly in hope and anticipation. In spite of the circumstances, I grew to love and cherish the new life growing within me. I loved babies, and part of me was looking forward to having one. I knitted a white sweater set for the baby, not knowing if it would be a girl or boy.

Paul had always known about our story because I had told him when he was very young. Talking about the past that morning brought it all back. He remembered that I had told him about the rape a long time ago, when he was in college, but he only vaguely remembered how the conversation had gone or why I had told him.

"I still can't believe I have a brother. How old was I when you were raped?"

"You were six months old," I said.

When Paul was three months old, doctors found the fontanel in his head was closing too quickly. They suggested surgery, and the news was shocking. I had worked with children who were challenged by a mental or physical handicap, so being aware that this occasionally happened through medical error at birth or during medical procedures increased my worry and fear. I did not want anyone to touch him without a second opinion. The Toronto Hospital for Sick Children had an excellent reputation, so I called a few friends who lived in the city and asked if I might live with them for a while. Honestly, I can't understand or remember how we ever got through that. Because of the great shame, judgement, and consequences attached to being an unwed mother in the '60s, I put a fake wedding band on my finger and the two of us flew to Toronto. Paul was an outpatient, and I would take him in every two weeks for head measurements and a weigh-in. After a few months, I was told that I could take him home because he was developing normally and was perfectly healthy. I quickly found a job in order to have money to buy a ticket to return home to New Brunswick. It was at that time that the rape happened and I became pregnant again.

"I do not want to talk about the rape today." I continued.

"I am sorry I didn't tell you about him sooner, but I don't believe I have ever forgiven myself for giving him up."

Paul did not question me, and we turned our attention back to Trevor. How did he end up in Vietnam? Did he ever come to Canada? Would we ever have the chance to meet him? Paul joked that we should just hop on a plane and go to Vietnam! We agreed that we would tell my daughter-in-law that evening, after she had time to settle in after a long day at work.

"How have the two of you spent your day?" she innocently asked when she arrived home.

Paul couldn't contain himself, and he just blurted out the news. Clearly, the story was overwhelming. Tears streamed down her cheeks as she embraced me.

Later that evening, I received a response email from Trevor answering the one I had sent to him telling him of my fears. It seemed that Trevor was also having his moments of fear and doubt. He had to have the courage to face the unknown. All his life, he had dreamt of finding me and had imagined the reunion as he would have wanted it to be. Now the unknown had grown from a dream to a reality. Did he really want to go through with this?

He had no idea of what he would find when he put in the request to the agency. He had no idea if I was dead or alive. He had no idea if I would acknowledge his existence or if I would want anything to do with him. He could not imagine who I would turn out to be. This was difficult for him too. His response was very honest.

June 27, 2016

Dear Yolande,

It is 2:43 a.m., and I have had another long day, but I will answer you out of respect for your concerns and worries.

I do not want or wish to make your life more difficult in any way. I have told you before that I simply want some answers to some questions. I know it is not easy facing me after what you have had to live through for forty-six years, but I do believe it is time to let it go. I am very straightforward and to the point in most things in life. I have no choice. It is the life I choose. I hope one day you will understand me as well as I understand you. :)

You say you are holding back… that has been obvious from the beginning. You say things are troubling you… I am responding for the same reason.

You could have tried to find me, and I think that is why I waited so long to find you. I didn't need to use the adoption agency to find you, I chose to do so… for you. To give you the choice to make another choice. If you think it is safer and easier to walk away… do it… I do not want to make you feel uncomfortable with me or with your past. I want you to want to do this in your heart with no more regrets. I will be fine; it is not the first time someone has left me. Your decision will open a door to the past or close it forever. Either way, I know what I must do when I wake up tomorrow morning. I have to make sure the twenty-two people who work for me get paid and we grow together in our businesses. I have to make sure they can feed their children and have work next month. I am truly sorry, but you are not the most important person in my life. You left me. Now it is time to make peace and grow or not... if you want me to disappear again, I can. It is truly up to you. After forty-six years... I believe I have the right to be honest too. I have no idea who you are, but I know I have love for you. Whether I ever meet you or not. You and no one is in danger.

Your children... well, again, it really all falls on your lap. It is not up to me. I am an email away from disappearing after you give me my bloodlines. As I told you, I don't really have much of a family, and I would love to know everyone in your family. I would love to come and have a BBQ and get to know all of you. :) I think it would be a great day. It would be great to have a reason to come back to Canada. It is your choice not mine. I have also told you... I have nothing to hide. I have no problem if you choose to tell your children about me or anything I have told you. I am also an open book, and this is a new chapter in life. :) I do get scared just like everyone else.

*My intent in this reply was not to make you feel
guilty. It was to set you free with no strings. Do what
is best for your children, not me. I am fine, trust me.*

Trevor

It was a blessing the email came while I was visiting Paul and
my daughter-in-law. I had read it privately first, but when I joined
them in the gazebo for a relaxing evening, I was not at all relaxed.
I tried speaking calmly and explaining that I had just received an
email from Trevor that said he didn't want to cause trouble for
me. That was all I could say. I felt the fear well up inside me. I
was afraid to lose him. I was afraid he was going to back out and
I would lose him again. Tears began to flow. My body felt tight,
and I trembled as I tried to hold myself together.

"Mom, would it be okay if I came to sit by you?" Paul asked
respectfully.

I nodded.

He asked, "May I put my arm around you?"

A flood of tears and sobbing was the answer. In his arms,
the fear, the hurt, and the shame I had felt many years ago from
being an unwed mother twice left my body. My daughter-in-law
sat quietly across from us seeming to hold all this in her heart. As I
rested in Paul's arms, red eyes and looking a mess, she smiled at us.

"This would make the most beautiful photo!" she said. Then
quickly added, "Don't worry—I won't do it!"

The tension was broken and we all laughed! I was grateful for
their understanding and their support.

After a few days, I was able to write back to Trevor.

June 30, 2016

Dear Trevor,

Thank you for your response. I really needed to hear that. All of it.

Thank you for giving me the chance to make another choice. The door to the past has been opened, Trevor. I opened it when I responded to the social worker, knowing in my heart that I would not abandon or reject you a second time. Knowing also that I would have to face my fears. You are not the cause of my fears, they come from my many experiences of the past. I do want to let it all go, but first I had to admit to myself and acknowledge that I was afraid. I had to get in touch with that fear, feel it, and let it go. It is okay, things are unfolding as they should. Little by little, I am getting to know you, and you are right, I know you very little. We both know each other very little. Because of that, we can only come to understand each other little by little. I can imagine how you must feel, but I do not want to make assumptions. So far, I believe that you are kind, hardworking, respectful, honest, and courageous. I also know that this is difficult for you too. I do not want you to disappear again. I believe if we continue to communicate in an honest way that we will understand each other more.

I want you to know that this journey we have embarked on has also brought me much joy. I thank you for initiating it; I just didn't know how. Please do not feel that you have to answer every time I

*write; I know that you have a heavy schedule, and
I can wait.*

Bonne nuit!

Yolande

In the months that followed, either one of us could have backed out because it was hard to face the past and to let it go. It meant that we had to be willing to see things in a different way and to dare believe that it could work out.

CHAPTER 7

You Have Another Brother

A fter I arrived back home in New Brunswick, I gathered my courage; I had more revealing to do. The time had come to tell my girls they had two brothers, not one. I ran the conversation through my mind many times over and in various ways. I rehearsed the opening line, but it didn't matter how I tried to change it around; the thought of speaking to them made me anxious. I didn't want to upset them or for them to hear the awful truth that their mom had given away a baby. Thinking about it caused me to feel an enormous weight on my shoulders and a pain in my heart.

It was July, and as much as I felt worried about telling Danielle and Natalie, I also wanted to let them know as soon as possible. I knew Paul would not mention the news to them before I had the chance to speak with them, but he was probably anxious to speak with his sisters about what he had learned. Also, the relationship between Trevor and I was growing; I was receiving regular correspondence from him, and I wanted to share it with them. I anxiously waited for Danielle to arrive home for her annual summer visit. In previous years she often arrived in July, however, that summer her trip was delayed because she had made plans for other travels.

Finally, I decided to speak to each of them separately and tell Natalie first since she lived close to home. I had no plan about when or how this would happen, but I knew I would have an opportunity soon because she would often drop by for a visit or

I would invite her for dinner. On one particular evening, after enjoying a light meal together, she seemed in no hurry to leave. We debated if it was too hot to take a walk to the wharf and watch the sun set. Natalie sat on the sofa and I in my comfy rocking chair nursing our cups of tea, and it occurred to me that this might be the opportunity to talk. I felt my heart racing as I gathered my courage and eased into the conversation.

"Have you heard from Danielle lately?" I asked.

"No, but last time we spoke, she seemed uncertain about her travel plans this summer."

"I know. I have been waiting anxiously for her to come home because I have something important to tell you. I was hoping to speak with both of you at the same time, but she is taking so long to come home this year, I guess I'll have to tell you first."

"Okay. What's going on, Mama?"

Natalie, being my youngest daughter, has a cute way of calling me Mama. It usually makes me smile, but this evening I didn't smile. She looked at me with a questioning frown.

"Remember a long time ago when you were a teenager and one day when I was worried for your safety, I told you I had been raped when I was younger?"

"Yes?"

"Well, what I didn't tell you was that I had a baby and had to give him away."

There was a moment of silence. I held my breath. Then tears filled her eyes.

"Oh, Mom! I think I'm going to need counselling!"

"I know," I said as I rose to get tissues and joined her on the sofa. I wrapped my arm around her shoulder and simply let the tears flow. Once I found my voice, I said, "Dear, you'll have to find someone else for that counselling. I can't help you, I'm too involved!"

We both laughed a little. We sat for a long while that evening. I answered her questions and gave her the information I had about Trevor.

Since Danielle does not live close to home we usually get in touch once a week on a video chat to catch up on the news—I enjoy my time with Danielle even if it is online. So at the beginning of the following month, I asked her again when she would be coming home. Normally, I do not ask so many questions, so she wondered what was going on. Finally, one day she told me that she may not be coming this summer because her plans for another trip were being delayed. She was still trying to work things out.

"But, Danielle, you have to come home, I have something important to tell you."

"Well, tell me now," she said.

"Not on a video chat. It's really important."

After some discussion, we agreed that if there was something important, she should know, and if there was a possibility of her not coming this summer, it might as well be said now.

And so it was.

I could only imagine what went through her mind as I told the story. There was a lot of silence from her end—not many words were spoken. I felt no judgement, only a lot of caring. With my oldest daughter, I was the one who broke down and cried. It was hard telling her when she was so far away, but I felt it was the right thing to do. Afterwards, I took comfort knowing all three now knew; they would be able to talk about it together and support one another.

Neither of my girls had any vivid memories of Trevor. Danielle vaguely remembered him from school, but he was three years older so they had no contact. Through later communication, we discovered that Trevor had attended the same college in Ottawa during the same year as Danielle. Luckily, they never met because another one of my fears had been that one of my daughters would show up with a new boyfriend who was my long-lost son!

CHAPTER 8

Getting in Touch with the Past

Hearing from Trevor and speaking with my children brought back memories of my pregnancy. I remembered that in an old album somewhere there was a photo of me, taken by a friend on my twenty-second birthday during my fourth month of pregnancy. After searching through many albums, I finally found it. I stared at the young lady in the photo. A few friends had made a birthday cake for me, and judging by its thickness, it looked more like one big brownie than a cake. It was covered in chocolate icing with a few candles planted here and there; definitely not twenty-two.

I did not look pregnant. I wore a fitted plaid dress, no more than a size ten. My long brown hair hung over my shoulders, and the smile on my face betrayed my feelings. I was just managing to breathe through one day at a time. The future seemed non-existent for it was impossible to imagine any further than that single day. Yet, I wore a lovely smile no different from any other birthday. As I looked at the photo, I wondered, *How could I possibly be so disconnected from reality? How could I look as though nothing was happening?* Perhaps it was a skill I had learned very young when my dad passed away. Time had stood still then also.

My mind backtracked to that ordinary morning in May of 1957. His death had happened very quickly. I was leaving the house to walk to school, and he was leaving to walk to work (not many people owned cars back then).

"Want to help me carry this ladder to Mr. Boudreau's house?" he asked.

Dad smiled a lot, and kindness showed through his eyes. The night before, Mom and Dad had been doing the spring cleaning. In those days it made sense to wash the walls, the drapes, the pictures on the walls—basically everything in the house—at least twice a year because the houses were heated with coal. Burning coal caused a fine black dust, called soot, to settle even on the ceilings.

I walked with him, me carrying the lighter end of the ladder, and then we parted. I don't remember his last words. I only remember that one morning he was there seeing me off to school and within the next two hours he suffered a heart attack and was gone. Until then, I didn't realize that a single second can change your whole life. One moment life is good, and then as the hand of the clock strikes that next second, your whole world changes. My world fell into shambles that morning, but I also learned from my mother's courage and determination; we must keep putting one foot in front of the other and move forward.

My father was forty years old when he died. Mom, who was thirty-eight, was left to take care of my fifteen-year-old brother, me at ten years old, and my sister who had just turned four a few months earlier. Mom was devastated. There was no insurance at that time, and the only benefit she could receive was a small allowance known as a widow's pension; not enough to support a family of four. So, Mom did what she had to do. She sold the house and sold or gave away most of what we owned. In September, my brother went away to a private school run by a religious order where he could earn his keep by working on the farm. It was only a four-hour drive away, but it felt much farther. My mother, sister, and I, along with our clothing, a few pieces of furniture, and a few of our favourite toys, moved in with an aunt who ran a boarding house in Moncton, a city about twenty-five kilometres from our former home.

As a ten-year-old child, I had no awareness of the hardship my mother was going through because I didn't see another tear after the funeral. She most likely saved the crying for moments when she was alone. I witnessed a strong woman dressed in black getting thinner and working long, hard hours in a grocery store. She was doing her best to make a normal life for her children. On Saturday evenings my little sister and I would be waiting anxiously for her to arrive home because Sunday was a day off and we could spend time together. She received her pay that day and would dig deep into the little brown envelope to give my sister and me fifteen cents each. With this small gift and the permission to cross the street, we went to Deluxe French Fries to get our treat of homemade fries served in a paper cone. This image is the most vivid happy memory I have of the few months after my dad passed away. I don't remember being told, but I remember clearly that we did not speak of my dad for fear of upsetting Mom or making her cry.

In the meantime, I was not doing well. I was grieving, but I also had a touch of depression, which is something that wasn't diagnosed back then. Mom knew there had to be a better way; a better life that might make us happier. The following May, she moved all of us back home to Shediac and went to work for a friend who owned a hairdressing shop. She later became a hairdresser and opened her own shop in our apartment so that she could be at home with us.

There were times, after the rape and during my pregnancy, when my feelings were similar. Like my mother, I couldn't escape my situation. I had to keep on walking, keep on going, and keep on living. On the inside I was devastated, living partly in denial and shame; the double shame of a second pregnancy as an unwed mother. Very few people knew what I was going through. On the outside, everything seemed normal. There were days when I actually felt hopeful. I loved babies, and I would sometimes imagine that all would be well. I didn't know how my story could have a happy ending, but there was hope deep in my heart. Hope that maybe I could keep the baby and have a happy family. Perhaps the photo of me, pregnant with Trevor, had been taken on one of those hopeful days.

Life continued in spite of everything. A former boyfriend, the young man I was seeing before I met Paul's father, came back into my life and we remained friends. He had been very supportive during the time I carried Paul and did not seem to think less of me for being pregnant. He was not ashamed to be seen with me and even visited me while I was in hospital when Paul was born. Soon afterward, we began dating again. He had finished university and found a good job, so we talked about getting married. In September when I returned from Toronto with Paul, he rented an apartment and furnished it for Paul and me to move into. He was still living with his parents, so he would work all day, come for dinner and spend the evening with us only to leave at 11:45 because the car (and the driver!) had to be home by midnight.

When I told him about the rape, he remained calm but found it difficult to respond. It was the kind of calm one exhibits after receiving a blow. There was nothing he could say, and though his body remained frozen, I could see the pain in his eyes. He said it did not change the way he felt for me, and we would be married soon. The following month, I found out I was pregnant from the rape. I cannot remember our exact conversation, but he continued coming home for dinner and going home to his parents at 11:45. I believed he really cared for me as much as I cared for him, but our lives had been turned upside down. We needed time to let things settle before making any major decisions.

In the meantime, we kept living as normally as we could. There were tense moments, of course, when we didn't know whether to express our affection or hold it back, not knowing what laid ahead of us. We went through some very sad and distressing moments where I would become overwhelmed and burst into inconsolable tears, but the respect and affection we felt for each other kept us together. There were the happy moments we spent as a make-believe family enjoying the small things in life—a Sunday drive, a fall fair, and many, many enjoyable hours fascinated by Paul as he discovered his environment. He was such a happy little boy who was blissfully unaware that our lives were rocky. He was intelligent, curious and quickly learned to crawl, stand, and empty the cupboards of all the pots and pans (one of his favourite things to do).

He had such a pleasant personality that he would attract attention when we took him out. One early evening when we went to the St. John Fall Fair, Paul was fascinated by the bright lights, the whirling rides and the music, sometimes clapping his hands with excitement. We stopped at a game table where my boyfriend tried to win a toy for him by trying to land rings on a bowling pin. I stood Paul on the counter so he could watch. He clapped and laughed each time a ring was tossed, but all three rings missed the pins. The circus worker was so taken by him that he gave him a big green and orange poodle just because he was so delightful.

Unfortunately, our happy make-believe family ended a few weeks before Christmas. I was wrapping gifts for my boyfriend's nephew and niece in the kitchen when he walked into the kitchen wearing a sombre look.

"You may not want to wrap those gifts," he said.

I turned to him with a puzzled look.

"I can't go through with this. It is killing my parents. You can have all the furniture and I will drive you anywhere you would like to go. I'm sorry I just can't do it. I will be letting the apartment go on January 1."

This time it was my turn to remain calm and unable to respond. There were no words, no motions to go through, just pain and a frozen stillness in my body. I continued wrapping the gifts.

On Christmas Eve, my then ex-boyfriend delivered me, Paul and all our belongings to my cousin Georgie's home where we remained until the following summer. Georgie and her husband Louis had four children of their own, yet they made room for Paul and me and my unborn baby. I had previously lived with them while working close to their home, and their children loved me and bounced around squealing with joy, so glad to have me back and with a new baby. Georgie was strong, but she knew the seriousness of the situation and was mostly silent as she helped me settle in. Whether she realized it or not, I drew from her strength on that day to continue breathing, to keep on going and doing what had to be done. Louis, a kind and sensitive man, tried his best to make the event pleasant. It was Christmas, after all. With tears in his eyes, he announced that we were taking Paul shopping to let him pick out a gift. Santa was coming to the house after supper and it would be unheard of if he didn't bring a gift for all the children. Ten-month-old Paul picked out a pink rubber cow as a favourite toy!

As these memories of my pregnancy unfolded, it was clear that this photo belonged to Trevor—it had been taken for him on that day long ago. Many photos had been lost or destroyed over the previous forty-six years, yet this one had been tucked away and safely kept, so I took this as a sign that it was meant for him to have. I sent the photo to Trevor through email and also mentioned to him that, out of curiosity, I searched the internet for the name of his restaurant and saw a photo of him with his staff. I wrote:

> *I am assuming it is you because the man in that photo looks very much like my family and reminds me of my father. Since I have seen a photo of you, I thought it would only be fair that I send you one of me. It was taken on my twenty-second birthday. It does not look like me now, but I thought you might like to have it. I was four months pregnant with you*

> *at the time. I am wondering if you also searched my
> name?*

Without responding to my question, Trevor sent a few photos of himself. I felt increasingly comfortable with revealing more about myself, so I sent him old photographs of my mom and dad which had been taken the year before my father passed away. Revisiting those photos made me nostalgic, and seeing Trevor's red hair often brought flashbacks of my father. In my memories, my dad was perfect. His smile and caring nature are what I remember the most, and I am told that I followed him around like a puppy. If he was in the garden, I was right by his side. I remember planting pansies along the sidewalk and dahlia bulbs under the bedroom window with him.

My dad loved children and would protect us from harm, even the perceived bad influence of the brand-new television sets that were invading homes in the fifties. My grandfather, who owned a small grocery store in our town, was one of the first to buy a large console floor model and install it in their living room. On Sunday evenings, the family, neighbours, and friends would gather and sit on chairs, stools, and on the floor to watch *The Ed Sullivan Show*. On Sunday afternoons it was customary for my aunts, uncles, and cousins to gather at my grandfather's house to spend the afternoon together. On one such afternoon while the women sat on the spacious verandah with the younger cousins and the men busied themselves smoking cigarettes and discussing their businesses and cars, a group of cousins decided to turn the television on. I have no memory of what came up on that black and white screen other than there was a lot of fighting and stressful music in the background.

"Turn that TV off!" yelled one of the uncles.

"No!" pleaded the older children.

My father marched in carrying a pail and my grandfather's cane. He grabbed an old plaid blanket from the sofa, wrapped it over his shoulders and parked himself in front of the TV screen, much to the protest of the children. Upside-down, the pail became a stool, the blanket a shawl and the cane a make-believe guitar. He began strumming and singing familiar songs, teasing the children and making jokes.

"Mr. MacDonald had a farm," he sang.

"No!" screamed the children. "It was Old—Old MacDonald!"

Within a few minutes the children joined in, and the television was turned off with no complaints. This was the kind man whom I knew as Dad.

I was a very curious child and often got into trouble. I once broke a basement window in our house by hitting it with a rock until it shattered because I wanted to know how hard a window had to be hit before it would break. I would walk in a ditch filled with water because I was curious to know how deep I needed to go before water went over the top of my boots. I remember borrowing my dad's grass shears to cut a hole in the neighbour's hedge and make a shortcut to my friend's house. When I got into trouble by being disobedient, his response was to engage me in a conversation and ask what was in my little head when I thought of doing whatever it was I had done. It was not an accusatory question; it was simply a sincere inquiry to which I would answer with a logical explanation and a promise not to do it again. I always kept my promises, but there were so many other questions that needed answering!

On cold winter nights, he would warm my spot in the bed by laying in it before I climbed in, then he would lead me in a very short prayer which I remember to this day. "Thank you, Lord, for all I have received today and forgive all the things I may have done wrong. Thank you for all that was given to everyone else today and forgive also what they did wrong." In the morning he would be up before any of us to stoke the coals in the furnace and turn on the stove in the kitchen where my brother and I would sit wrapped in blankets before getting dressed and ready for school.

Once the kitchen was warmed up, Mom would come out with the baby and prepare breakfast.

Did my dad do these things regularly or perhaps only once or twice? I will never know, but these are the memories I cherished after I lost him. His image, I am aware, was embellished by the fact that he died when I was ten years old. I never had to take him off the pedestal by living with him through my teen years. If I had, I likely would have noticed that he was only human. Memories, I have learned, reflect our own truth and the way we experienced the events, not always the facts exactly as they were.

Trevor very much resembled his grandfather. Besides having red hair, through his letters I sensed that he was kind, caring, and he loved children. I had to be careful not to project onto him what belonged to my dad, but the one thing they certainly shared was that I had lost them both. The fact that Trevor brought back memories of my father was soothing to me and calmed the fears of meeting him. However, I was also very conscious that I needed to get to know Trevor for Trevor and not as a way of resurrecting the memory of dear sweet Dad.

CHAPTER 9

Being Vulnerable

Trevor and I slowly formed a relationship as the bridge of communication he hoped for in his first email gradually came into being. I let him know that Paul, Danielle, and Natalie now knew about him and that the conversations had gone well.

As September arrived and a new school year began, students and teachers returned to their normal schedules. I have always loved the freshness and nostalgia of the fall—the crisp, clean air of autumn brings back memories of preparing my children for the new school year. As they tried on last year's fall and winter clothing, I was amazed to notice how much they had grown. Buying new clothes, lunchboxes, and school bags, and their anticipation of meeting new teachers and seeing all their friends always brought excitement to the air. I cherish these memories.

At the same time, my thoughts that year went to Trevor. I had not had the privilege of creating those kinds of memories with him as a child. I wondered if the school year was the same in Vietnam, so I wrote to him saying I was thinking about him and wondering how it all happened where he lives.

> *If it is the beginning of a new year at your learning centre, it must be a super busy time for you. I wish you a very happy and good year with your staff and students.*

It was now three months since we had begun writing. When the answers to my emails did not come back immediately, I sometimes still felt vulnerable. Doubts crept into my mind. During these times, the chatter in my head could easily tip toward a negative outcome and become destructive. Maybe he would never write again. Or perhaps I was going too fast. Perhaps I should not have sent that photo, or maybe I said something hurtful? I made a conscious effort to remind myself that making assumptions did not serve me well. I encouraged myself to be patient even as I waited impatiently for his reply.

I pondered opening up to friends and sharing the news with the rest of my family. I knew it could be difficult to draw the curtain aside and let my friends and family see what was going on in my life. Telling them I had a son who was searching for me meant talking about the past, answering many questions, talking about the experience of being raped and about leaving the baby behind. These were traumatic events that were extremely difficult to look at and bring out into the open. After telling my children, I thought I was ready to open up. I had no plans as to how or when this might happen, or who I would speak to first, but I simply had a feeling that opportunities would present themselves. When they did, I would no longer hide—I would simply speak the truth.

The first of these occasions was at a restaurant with a friend with whom I had already shared part of the story long ago when she was going through some difficulties in her own life. It was a beautiful fall day, still warm enough to be sitting in the gazebo of the restaurant enjoying lunch. The subject came up some time between finishing our pizza and starting on dessert.

"Feels like ages since we have had time to talk. Anything new in your life?" she asked.

It was an ordinary question. Generally, I responded with something like, "Just the usual. A lot of walking on the beach, visiting with a few friends and family, and a couple of day trips." She was in no way prepared to hear my news that day.

"To tell you the truth, it has been a very moving and exciting summer. My son, the one I gave up forty-six years ago, found me. I received a letter from him and we have been corresponding for a few months now."

The dessert sitting on the plates in front of us suddenly lost its importance. Tears welled up in her eyes. Hand on her heart, she embraced the news.

"I am so happy for you; I am so happy for you. I am so happy for him!"

No sooner had I spoken these words when I began to see spots and flashes in my left eye. At first, I did not pay much attention, blinking and rubbing my eye to make the spots and threads go away. I did not tell my friend—who is a nurse—what was going on. Instead, I decided to go home and rest, but that did not help. The flashing in my eye got progressively worse. By ten o'clock that evening, I had to ask my daughter to drive me to the hospital. It turns out I had a retinal tear requiring laser surgery. I did not think the eye problem had anything to do with the conversation and figured it was just a coincidence. After the surgery, the ophthalmologist assured me all was well, the damage had been repaired, and no special precautions needed to be taken.

Two days later, I was driving a friend to an appointment and again, the subject of having a son finding me came up. Slowly, spots began to appear in the same eye. Frightened and worried that my eye was bleeding from the inside, I called my ophthalmologist. This time it was even worse, and I was two hours away from home. The ophthalmologist asked if I could make it back home.

"I will see you at eight o'clock tomorrow morning," she said.

Darkness had begun to fall and it was raining. I drove home able to see out of only one eye. In the morning, after checking the area of the first surgery and confirming that everything looked normal, the doctor said this was unusual. There was a new retinal tear that also needed to be repaired. I did not share with the doctor what was happening in my life at the time, however, I had read many articles that talked about the link between our thoughts and emotions and some illnesses or physical conditions in the body. Could this be more than a coincidence? Had my body been manifesting my fears of looking into the past and speaking about the events I had kept in the dark all these years? I will never know for sure, but it's possible.

Talking openly about my experiences became easier with time, and the judgements I had feared did not manifest. Friends and family were very touched by the story, sorry to hear what had happened, and happy—so happy—that my son had found me. There were sometimes tears, always questions, but mostly awe at what was unfolding.

My life was beginning to return to an almost normal routine, and I was committed to facilitating a session in September at a small retreat centre called La Solitude, a place that was near and dear to my heart. I had retreated there when I was twenty-eight and trying to pull my life together. I had often found comfort, strength, and healing during those challenging years.

La Solitude is situated on several acres of land in Memramcook, New Brunswick. It is a beautiful, serene, peaceful place where people attend retreats and workshops on topics concerning personal and spiritual growth. Amongst the giant old trees, all paths lead to the waters of the Petitcodiac River. I could spend hours in silence watching the tides roll in from the Bay of Fundy, which has the highest tides in the world. It is estimated that 160 billion tonnes of sea water flow in and out of the bay twice a day. What a powerful symbol for both receiving and letting go!

Nestled among the trees, fifteen rugged cabins host individuals who come to rest, relax, and reconnect. On a hill overlooking the water stands the Tabor, a meeting place. All the buildings on the grounds were built by missionary priest Father Bujold, who had worked for fifteen years in India. Having been exposed to solitude as he walked many kilometres to reach distant villages, he came to understand the value of being alone in nature and in silence.

Upon his return to Canada, he built La Solitude so folks would have a peaceful place to retreat from the busyness of everyday life and reconnect with nature and life within themselves.

I had benefited from Father Bujold's help earlier in my life when I spent that week in silence at his retreat. I was searching for answers and seeking help because I believed there was something terribly wrong with me. I was married with two beautiful children, and I had a good life. However, there were times when I was alone, especially in the early morning and late in the evening when everyone was asleep, when I would lie awake with tears rolling down my face for apparently no reason. I had accumulated so much self-loathing and often repeated *What is wrong with you? Stop crying for nothing* to myself. I had seen a doctor and a psychiatrist, but I did not want to take tranquilisers and nothing seemed to help.

My first meeting with Father Bujold lasted no more than ten minutes when I briefly and bluntly told him the story of my life. As he listened, I saw caring, kindness, and understanding in his eyes. He was a man of few words, but the words he spoke remain deeply imprinted in my mind.

This is what I remember:

> Life within you is very strong. Have you ever seen the poster of a flower or a blade of grass pushing through and breaking the pavement? You are like that; there is a force inside you that wants to live at all costs. There is nothing wrong with you; you are not crazy. You, on the contrary, are very resilient. Events in your life have been demolishing, just as a hurricane can demolish a house. But the foundation is still there. We just have to rebuild. I will help you. To become happy, Yolande, you need three things. First you need to clean up your past, deal with the difficult

> emotions, and release them. Next you need to
> discover who you truly are. Finally, you need to
> dare to live your life, you need to fly. You will
> go far.

I had no idea what the word resilient meant, but I had seen the poster showing a dandelion breaking through the cement pavement. For some reason I believed him. He gave me hope because he was wise and drew his wisdom from life experiences. He radiated peace, he was compassionate and kind, yet firm. He believed in humanity and had a great understanding of human behaviour. He was generous and caring, encouraging life and growth in all who came to him for help. He believed in me and believed I was capable. He spoke of God, a loving, non-judgemental God. In India, Father Bujold had been a dentist, a doctor, an educator, a priest, a psychologist, a carpenter—whatever people needed, he became that person. In Canada, he shared what he had experienced in silence with humility. He gave his presence and his attentive ear to whomever needed it. I followed his instructions and did the work for many years.

Father Bujold passed away in 2010, so to give back some of the life and hope I received from him, I volunteered my services at La Solitude. I felt I was a living example of the training and education La Solitude embodied, and I was now capable of giving back. I was to deliver a session on the subject of inner peace. I had given similar workshops to groups of people looking for personal or spiritual development, but preparing this session was quite a challenge given what was going on in my own life. I had been pushed to test my theories, use my own tools, and choose to live in a learning mode, observing the process within myself. My experience of inner peace had shifted from believing that it meant being calm most of the time to understanding that it could also be found during tumultuous times. I noticed that when I could accept the situation as it was and accept the emotions that showed up inside me, I could find peace. When I fought against the feelings and emotions that rose inside, I would lose my inner peace.

As I prepared my session, I wondered when or if I would receive more news from Trevor. He had not yet replied to the note I had sent him about the beginning of the school year. Then one day, the reply arrived. As I read his email, I understood that we were both feeling vulnerable.

September 6, 2016

> *Hi, I am sorry for not responding yet. It is hard to reply at this time. I think it may even be harder for me now to absorb all of this than I thought. All of this has really changed my life, and it is difficult to speak so openly about myself. I really am a very private person, and I focus on what I need to do. I have a lot of people depending on me every day, and I want to succeed in every way. Sometimes I am afraid of success because I worry about the responsibilities that come with it. I can see a distance between my father and me now; even though he says he does not feel threatened by my contacting you. Please be patient with me… I will find my way, and I will find you :) Thank you for your email… it makes me happy to hear from you. :)*

> *Trevor*

I was not certain how to respond, but my intuition told me to tread carefully. I sensed that he needed to have some space to work things out.

September 11, 2016

Hi Trevor,

I hear you. Sounds like your plate is quite full, and that is good. Please don't worry about finding time to write when you are so busy. I remember the last thing that you said to me in the first letter that you wrote to me (through the social worker). You said that you knew why you are here and that was: to help people. I believe that you are doing that; it is your priority, and that is good. I am glad when you do write, but I wouldn't want it to be another stress, like another thing you "have to do."

I understand how all of this can feel overwhelming for you. When you decided to look for me, you had no idea of what to expect. I am glad that you did. Please take all the time you need to absorb things as they come up for you. I am happy just knowing that you are there, that you had good parents, and that you are doing well. That is more than I could ever have wished for. There is no rush for anything else. I hope I didn't worry you when, in one of my emails, I mentioned that I like to travel and said maybe someday I would visit Vietnam. I didn't mean anytime soon. I believe that things will happen as they are meant to; there is lots of time.

If it makes you happy to hear from me, then I will continue to write. Don't feel obliged to answer all the time. Just, once in a while, let me know if you're still there, and that will make me happy.

Take care

Yolande

This time the response came quickly.

September 13, 2016

Yolande,

I still feel a lot of secrecy from you. I guess I just need to read our past emails. I have a bad habit of not trusting people… but often I am right. I don't know why I am so defensive with you. Forgive me. We two live in very different worlds. I do believe you are honest with me. It is just a habit not yet forgotten in my world. I hope one day you can understand me. That will not be easy after all this time. I do promise one thing… I will never bring you harm. I can promise this. It will just take time to feel comfortable, and as I said before, it is the same for all of us knowing how I came to be.

I do love hearing from you and Paul. I sent Paul a very long email just now. I had a free morning today. I wanted to write, and I wanted to talk. I hope you both share my emails as I am sure you do. I think I wrote too much to him. I guess I just want you all to know me before you continue any other relations with me. I am not an angel, and you need to know this. You are hard to compute for me… funny with Paul I do not worry what he thinks of me when I share my life as I do with you. I do not like this feeling of worrying what people think of me.

I want him to understand me, and I want him to share in the same way out of common respect. I told Paul I buried my mother, and it is hard to think I may have another. I know your heart is good, but I also know you will only tell me what you think is right. Sometimes I think forgetting you and what I have done is better for everyone involved. I do not want to bring hardship or pain to any of you, but I am who I am, and I cannot communicate with you without telling you how I feel and how I became who I am. This is one of the hardest things I have had to do. Knowing me will not be easy for you or your family. I am a very determined and passionate man. I will continue to do what I do in my world. I do not want to hurt you in any way. I hope you can understand that.

Trevor

I was putting the final touches on the session I was about to deliver on the weekend at La Solitude and preparing to leave. Before I had time to respond another email arrived...

September 15, 2016

Hi Yolande,

Forgive me. I am emailing you again because I feel badly about the last email I sent you. I was talking in circles, not being honest with myself or you, and I'm sure none of it made much sense. Humm...

A few nights ago, after everyone had gone to bed, I decided to sit back and reflect on what I was doing and what needs to be done next as I normally do in the evenings. After having a few drinks, I felt that it was time to write back to Paul. As I started thinking about the two of you and reading his previous email, I started feeling down and I guess a little depressed. Maybe even feeling a little sorry for myself. It is not like me to be this way, but to be honest, it has bothered me to know how I came to be. Also, when Paul told me the first time we met we had been in a fight. Wow!!! I never expected all this, and it caused me to be a little emotional. I think this is where I got into saying... I don't want to hurt anyone, even though I have already brought pain. I understand there is nothing I can do about any of it, but it is awkward. At that time in my life getting into fights and being kicked out of school was a regular occurrence. I still do not remember Paul.

I wrote Paul, and it was getting very late and I was unfortunately getting quite emotional with the continuing drinking. I told him a lot, and I wrote for a couple hours. Looking back on that night I know I told him some very personal things, and I think that is fine. He asked what I had done and where I had gone since high school. I told him the truth.

I know why I feel uneasy with you. It's all about the secret you had for forty-six years and how I came to be. I had prepared myself for decades to expect the worst so that nothing would phase me. I told myself the worst stories as I approached my time to face you. I told myself that the only thing that was important was to learn my bloodline regardless of anything bad. I told myself it was very possible that neither of you would want anything to do with me. I told myself that maybe meeting you and my brother would just be a second possibility. Even if deep down inside I knew I wanted more. I never thought about how we would communicate or how I would feel reading your emails. I told myself and convinced myself knowing my bloodline was the only important thing. I tried to keep it all simple. How silly. My mission in finding you was simple, and anything else was luck. Anything else was just a dream and worth only thinking about from time to time. For as long as I can remember I have always said to myself, my family is the one that I will build. Now I hope you will be of that family. That is why I am here in Vietnam and why I believe financial freedom is that key. What I do makes me happy, but where I am does not. What worries me now is what you said. You said, "I will answer you as truly as I can, except for my secret that I kept for forty-six years." I can imagine why your daughters have not emailed me yet; I can image that they may think I am a monster. You said you had to see a psychologist and you were afraid I would make you think of him. I think it is now both our pain, and I think it is only us together that can let it go. It worries me that you may not tell me who he was, what his name was or how you met him. This is where I am now, lost again and getting emotional, because giving me what I need causes you pain. I said I would not hurt you, but I already have. I believe closure comes through you, and I need to know who he was and where he came from. My birth father may have been a monster, but I need to know that there is more to me than him. I need to know there was some good on some side of where he came from. I know I need you to get past this with me… I don't want to feel lost anymore. I want peace.

I will understand if I do not hear from any of you again. I am sorry, I really am. But I need to know the truth. I hope you can find the strength to share our rough beginning one final time.

Love Trevor

September 16, 2016

Dear Trevor,

Thank you for being so honest. I just want to let you know that I have received your email this morning as I checked my messages before going out the door. I am leaving for the weekend and will not have access to internet. So, I just wanted you to know that I have read your email and that I find nothing shocking or disturbing about what you shared. On the contrary, I think that if we both keep on communicating how we feel and where we are at, that we will be OK. I will be answering you soon after the weekend.

Yolande

September 21, 2016

Hi Trevor,

Hope you were able to get some sleep after writing all those long emails. No, Paul and I do not share your emails so if there is something that you want me to know, I guess you will have to tell me directly.

I have to say that I am finding it very difficult to communicate by writing because in writing it is so easy to make interpretations. I used to give sessions on communication when I was working, and I would teach that in a written message we are only getting, I think it is ten to fifteen percent of the message that the other person is trying to tell us. Another thirty to thirty-five percent comes through our tone of voice, and all the rest is communicated by body language. So, you see, as much as we are trying to make each other understood, there is a lot of the message we are not getting even if we are being honest. However, that is what we have for now, so we will make the best of it.

I will start by saying please do not worry about what I said… and you quoted me in saying, "I will answer you as truly as I can, except for my secret that I kept for forty-six years." I believe if you continue reading, I went on to say… I am a very honest person (or something like that). Anyhow, when I mentioned "…the secret that I kept for forty-six years," I was referring to you, Trevor. Some people knew that I had been raped, but very few knew that you were born; that was my big secret. Perhaps because I had never forgiven myself for giving you up, even if I felt in my heart that it was the best thing for both of us, I thought others would never be able to forgive that either.

I agree with you that it is difficult to speak of your beginnings. It must have been a terrible shock to you to hear this. When I heard you were looking for me, I did not know how I would ever be able to tell you that I was raped. So, the social worker said he would tell you. I'm sorry it had to be that way. I wish I would have had the strength to tell you myself, but I couldn't do it. Now I wish we could talk about this in person. Forty-six years ago, I believe we were both victims that night. You were a totally innocent baby. Yes, I was afraid to see or meet you because I had no idea how I would react when I met you. You see, I do not remember what your biological father looks like at all. But I knew that the fear was registered in my body and it might be triggered if you resembled him. I was afraid that whatever my reaction would be that you might feel hurt or rejected again. And I did not want that to happen. I also did not want to feel that pain again. You are absolutely right in saying, "I think it is now both our pain, and I think it is only us together that can let it go." I cannot tell you much about him. I had only been working at a new job for less than a week when it happened. He was my shift supervisor. I know nothing about him. He does not know that you exist. I honestly have no recollection at all of what he looked like. I left the city soon after and put it all behind me. You were born in my home province of New Brunswick.

Trevor, I hope someday that we will be able to sit together and talk about this. I am willing to be very open with you. I have come to forgive him because it was not healthy for me to hold all that inside me. With counselling and in learning psychology I have understood that he must not have been a happy man because people who are happy do not hurt others. I also do not want to label people. I have learned that people are not "alcoholics" or "rapists" or whatever, they are first a person. A person who made bad choices and hurt others. This helped me to let it go. Your biological father was not necessarily a bad person, but he did make bad choices. I understand that it is part of your past, but you are not him. You are you, and I will be happy to meet you.

I also want to reassure you that your sisters do not think of you as a monster... that thought belongs to you in your head; please let it go and do not hurt yourself needlessly. You have enough pain as it is. Your sisters are just figuring out their own stuff. Just allow them time; they have both told me they want to write to you it just hasn't happened yet. You know, all of this coming out in the open has brought up many unresolved things from your past, my past, and my other children's pasts. I still believe this is a blessing. It is giving all of us a chance to look at the truth and to heal. We cannot change the past, but we can accept that "what is, is" and make the best of the future one day at a time. So, my dear, that is all I can write for tonight. I do want to tell you that I, too, already feel love for you. How could I not? I gave you birth.

Take good care of yourself, what will be will be.

Yolande

CHAPTER 10

Growing the Relationship

Trevor and I got through that difficult but very honest period of sharing. The relationship was growing, but we were each growing personally in our own way. Life has a funny way of presenting opportunities when we are ready to accept them. Long before Trevor contacted me, I had registered for a session, called Healing the Heart, in October 2016 at the Chopra Center in California. I knew of the Center because Natalie and I went there in 2013, shortly after my retirement. The Chopra Center felt like an invitation to move forward with my life, find new purpose, and pursue my evolving interest in meditation. The following year we once again signed up for a women's retreat where one of the themes was self-love and acceptance. We were asked to look into a small hand-held mirror while Gordon Lightfoot's "The First Time Ever I Saw Your Face" played in the background. I have no idea where the tears came from, but they poured out profusely. Intuitively, I knew I still needed to heal somewhere deep in my heart. My intuition also told me to sign up for Healing the Heart, so I should have expected it would be perfect timing!

I arrived at the session alone this time because Natalie and I agreed that this session had to be done individually. The session was based on Dr. David Simon's book *Free to Love, Free to Heal.* Dr. Simon was the co-founder of the Chopra Center and was a physician, now passed, who had a great respect and love for life. He believed that emotional freedom is at the heart of true healing.

Here, in his own words, is why he wrote the book and later went on to develop the session that I was about to attend. "I wrote *Free to Love, Free to Heal* as a guide to help you identify and release the impediments to your ability to give and receive love. This book will show you how to recognize the parts within you that hurt and apply the balm of loving to promote emotional and physical healing." I was so fortunate to be there at this time in my life. I truly wanted to recognize the parts within myself that hurt, and I wanted to heal. I was ready.

After the facilitators took care of the introductions and instructed us on how we would proceed, we were shown a short silent film. The black and white cartoon portrayed a character hauling a heavy trunk and in spite of the pain it caused him, he was not ready to let it go. As I sat in silence and watched, I recognized the trunk symbolized my past – stories holding shame and hurts tucked away for no one to see, old beliefs that I adopted as my own, paradigms that no longer served me – all neatly stored. The message was clear: I needed to let go of my past. I understood how easy it was to lug old stories and secrets and how difficult it is to let them go, even if they cause pain. It's almost like an addiction. How would I live without my story? Who would I be? Would it be possible to let go the unworthy story and become free to love, even myself?

The exercises that followed turned out to be revealing, especially the exercise on forgiveness. I discovered that the person I most needed to forgive was myself. Journaling was the tool we used. As I wrote about an event or situation where I had been hurt by another and viewed it from a distance as an observer, it was helpful to take a certain distance from my pain and understand it a bit more. Later I wrote about a time where I had caused hurt or harm to another person, again as an observer. I understood that I had not meant to harm the other I was acting out of fear or hurt, trying to get my needs met. This helped me understand that we have all been hurt in our lives and we have all hurt someone at one time or another. I was not a bad person, as I had been led to believe. I began to feel compassion towards myself and others. I felt judgement slip away. It also freed me from the heaviness of anger and blame I was feeling toward others.

Meanwhile back in Vietnam, Trevor was busy with his work and becoming more open to sharing parts of his life with me through email. He told me about the conversational English he taught to all who were eager to learn, from kindergardners up to adults. He talked about preparing programs, creating books, and teaching the students about other cultures, and he shared his excitement about the Halloween party he was planning for the children. He mentioned that at Christmas he would be Santa and had ordered a special suit made for the occasion. He spoke about making learning English fun for the children as he integrated the lessons into everyday activities such as making pizza and playing soccer. He mentioned creating jobs for people to help feed their families and that he dreamt of creating opportunities which would last longer than he would in that country.

Although I felt I didn't deserve any of the credit for who he had become, I felt proud of who he had grown to be and of the work he was doing. Little by little, we were getting closer and developing a certain level of trust. Our email greetings from May to September gradually changed from *Hi Trevor* to *Dear Trevor*; from *Yolande* to *Dear Yolande*.

November was my birthday month. As cards, flowers, and gifts poured in from my friends, family, and three children, it was important to share this news with Trevor.

November 22, 2016

Dear Trevor,

Online, I have just found a video of last year's Christmas party at your learning centre. I am really impressed, proud, and emotional. Even if we have never met, I feel that there is so much of me in you. I love children, and for many years when I was young, I ran kindergartens and day-care centres. Even if I feel I don't deserve any of the credit for who you are, my heart is still bursting with pride as I watch this video over and over again. I believe this will be one of my greatest Christmas gifts. I hope you don't mind; I will be showing it off just like a mom goes around showing off a new child. I am so anxious to meet you in person. Just for fun I am sending you a photo of me with my kindergarten class taken about forty years ago! One of my students posted it online some time ago.

This month I will be seventy years old! I can't believe it… I sure don't feel it, whatever one is supposed to feel at seventy. This year has been incredible, and I plan to make the next ten the best ever! I will be leaving for Florida next week; I have a friend who invites me and we share rent. I will continue to be available by email, so I will keep in touch.

Congratulations, Trevor, on all your great work.

Love,

Yolande

November 23, 2016

Dear Yolande,

You have many kind words :).

It makes me happy that you are happy. I, too, hope to meet you in person as soon as possible. I want to know everything about you.

I want to wish you a very happy birthday. I wish I could be there to enjoy this time with you. I am sure we will be seeing you on birthdays to come :).

Florida will be great I am sure... you are lucky to have such good friends.

Thank you again for your kind words,

Trevor

I will write longer soon. Still just so busy with work...

Seven months after Trevor and I shared our first emails, Christmas was approaching, and I really wanted to meet him. Christmas is one of those special times during the year where the heart gets softer and we think of people we love, near or far. They all have a special place in our hearts. Having spent many, many wonderful Christmas seasons with Natalie, Danielle, and Paul as they grew up, it always brought me happiness to be with them at that time of the year as they became adults. At times I could still picture them as little children, eyes sparkling, waiting for the magic of Christmas to happen. They didn't realize they were the magic.

As I let myself drift in the memories of Christmases gone by, I pictured Paul—red cheeks, almost lost in his large snowsuit; he was the little boy who was so excited to go outside first thing on Christmas morning to try out his brand-new snow shovel. I remembered Danielle at two years old—blonde hair, blue eyes. She was the perfect child to play the role of baby Jesus in a Christmas play. After all, this was the way baby Jesus was often portrayed in the Western world even if he was Jewish and probably had darker skin and hair. The Christmas play had been presented for parents and friends at the kindergarten that I ran in our finished basement. Danielle, in her long blue nightgown, laid angelically in a wicker bassinet on the floor. The room was still as the narrator read the story. Two adorable little girls sat quietly in sheep costumes, and the shepherds waited attentively for their cue in the background. Suddenly, Danielle got impatient, sat up and ordered the shepherds, "OK, you shepherds, bwing me my pwesants!" The audience roared with laughter. Then there was Natalie. So precious she was, with her big brown eyes, dressed in her quilted yellow jacket and fur hat. She made the first page of the local newspaper, the *Moncton Times and Transcript* that year. The photographer captured her as she watched her first Santa Claus parade filled with awe. So many special Christmas memories!

I had no such memories of Trevor at Christmas. Through the years, my heart had remembered him, wondered where he was, and hoped that he was being well taken care of. Then I would shut that door so as not to feel the great hurt of leaving a child behind, and fall into despair. This was how I guarded my mental health.

Perhaps Trevor remembered and imagined me at Christmas time in his childhood and as he grew into adulthood. For, to my great surprise, early in December it was Trevor who sent the first email mentioning Christmas. It was addressed to his siblings and me.

December 7, 2016

Hi :),

I just wanted to say that I am very happy to have received your emails, and it means a lot to me.

Thank you for your time and words. They mean a lot more than you can know.

It has been an eye-opener for sure. I am very proud of all of you. I mean this… I had no idea what or who I was going to meet when I found you or my mother. Strange and exciting for all I guess, and I hoped it would be all good. I did worry for years, that I may be bringing trouble to you and your family for knowing my presence, but our mother has been very supportive of my efforts and tells me she is happy to know me. Of course, I am happy to hear this and will continue to send emails.

I wanted you to know that all is good here in Vietnam, and I look forward to meeting all of you someday. I mentioned to our mother that the learning centre had a Halloween trick-or-treat run here in Cam Pha, and it was a huge success. There will also be a Christmas party and Santa will be visiting. All is well here. The restaurant is relatively new but growing.

I think emails make it hard to communicate, and I wanted you to all know… I talk with my (adoptive) father regularly (video chat). So, if anyone wants to talk a little more, here is my online contact.

I will email you all again soon… I'm sure you are just as busy as or busier than I. I wanted to make sure to wish you all a Merry Christmas if I do not hear from you before then :).

Merry Christmas everyone :).

P.S. If you talk to my youngest sister, please let her know I look forward to hearing from her.

I was in Florida when I received the email and wasted no time in writing back.

December 11, 2016

Hi Trevor,

Thank you for the lovely email. I was very happy reading your message. I have forwarded it to Natalie. She said she would be writing to you soon… she has a lot going on in her life right now.

Thank you for the Christmas wishes. How is the Santa suit coming along? I have been thinking about your offer to video chat with you. Many times, it had crossed my mind also, but I was hoping to meet you in person first. I think it would be very hard to see you and not be able to hug you!

You know, Trevor, if you have the time and the means to get here you are very welcome to come and visit me in Florida. My friend Vi, who invites me to share the mobile home, would be so happy to meet you. She had only one son and he died of cancer two years ago. She thinks I am so lucky to have received the gift of another son. So, seriously, the offer is there.

Take care,

Yolande

December 12, 2016

Hello my Dear,

Santa is coming along great, and I will send you pictures soon.

I, too, hope I can visit soon. It would be great to come see you in Florida. I am happy for you… that you are in Florida enjoying life. It really makes me feel good that you are happy and well. It is something I worried about for many years.

I don't want you to think about online video conferencing… I agree with you. I, too, want to see you in person. It has been a long time waiting for a hug :). I have no hard feelings, and I want us to have many years together :). It's not every day one can say they found another mother. It will take time, but it is wanted :). I just want you to be there now and be my friend. I miss my mother very much… she understood and truly supported me. I wish you could have met her :(. She was very special… she wanted to meet you very much, and she also said I should find you.

I really wish I could visit you in a warm Florida… but I can't leave this place at this time. I am just responsible for too many things at the moment. I truly hope next year I can come visit and spend time with you all. It would be amazing for sure :).

Love Trevor

December 16, 2016

Dear Trevor,

Your mom sounds like she was very special to you. I am sorry for your loss, and I am sorry I will never get to know her. Maybe I did meet her while I lived in the same community a long time ago. I am anxious to hear all about her.

All I can say is thank you. Thank you for finding me. Thank you for sharing your thoughts and feelings. Thank you for just being you.

Have a very happy Christmas!

Sending you a virtual hug till we meet! ☺

Yolande

When January came along, I dared to ask Trevor a very important question.

Dear Trevor,

Would you allow me to see you if I came to Asia? Just asking... I often wonder if you live near a port city. I could take a cruise and maybe you could visit with me for a day. I'm not saying I could or would anytime soon, but the thought has been on my mind since you have contacted me.

I was moved by his answer.

> *My dear long-lost Yolande. Of course, you can travel*
> *this way. One day to see you would not be enough.*

Time passed, and we did not speak of the possibility of a trip
again until April 2017. Then one day I opened an email with the
subject line "Try this for a cruise... maybe?" He had sent me a
link to a cruise line that would be stopping in his area. A smile
immediately lit up my face. *He does want me to come!* In spite of
all the emails we had shared and all his kind and forgiving words,
it was still difficult for me to believe that he would really want to
meet me. Forty-six years of not daring to dream while living in
fear and denial made it difficult for me to believe a real in-person
relationship was possible. This step from him led me to believe it
truly was, so I slowly began gathering information about cruises
that travelled to his area.

April 20 was always one of the most difficult days of the year
for me. It was a day when I could not turn off the memories. It
was Trevor's birthday. My heart was heavy and sad on this day, but
no one noticed because I was very good at hiding what was going
on inside me. I always allowed myself a little time alone, usually
in the morning when I woke up, to remember and experience
the sadness. Once alone in my room in the evening, I sent him
blessings and good wishes. Sometimes I tried to imagine what he
might look like at that age, and I always imagined him doing well.
Then I would return to the present and be grateful for all that I
did have. This year was different!

> *Dear Trevor,*
>
> *For the first time I can wish you a happy day on*
> *your birthday! And for the first time I can say that*
> *April 20 is a happy day for me. Every year I would*
> *think of you and wonder how you were, where you*
> *were, and in my heart, I would send you love and*

blessing hoping you were well and happy. This year,
I can actually say that to you.

I do hope you have received my card. I wish you a
wonderful day, and hopefully we will meet this year.

Sending love,

Yolande

In his answer Trevor let me know, with kind words, how meeting this year would not be possible. He had hoped he could come to Canada for a visit, but with all new contracts and a heavy workload at the learning centre, it was not possible to leave. Next year would be best. Interesting, isn't it, how one can believe that the other person has the same thoughts and plans in their mind as we have in ours? I had assumed with the email giving me a link for a cruise that it was okay if I came to visit. All along I was thinking that I would soon be visiting him in Vietnam and he was thinking of possibilities to come to Canada. After a week or so, I brought up the subject again, this time being much clearer about my intentions.

Hi,

Trevor, I do not want to cause you any extra stress
but, what about if I came to visit you? I know this
is a big thing, but I often wonder if it would be
possible. I also wonder if you would be able to take
a little time off in spite of all the work that keeps
you busy.

I have thought of several ways I could do this. So far,
just thoughts and dreams, but let me tell you about

it and then you can tell me what you think. Perhaps one of the children might make a short trip with me. We would fly into Hanoi and stay in a hotel, and you could come to visit. Is Hanoi close to you? Or I could take a cruise with a friend, and when we stop close to where you are you could meet me. Another possibility would be to join a group that is going to tour Vietnam. I would be fine to travel with them alone. One tour that I have found leaves in October and would be in your area for a few days.

So, I know you are very busy and work, work, work. I'm just wondering if you think it would be a good idea for me to go there. I want you to be honest with me and tell me how you feel about it. If you prefer to wait until you can come to Canada maybe next year that is OK also. I am anxious to meet you, but I understand your situation and I can wait. Think about it for a while and when you have time let me know your thoughts. I will follow your lead. I just want you to know that I am looking forward to meeting you.

In the meantime, I send you hugs,

Yolande

The reply came back immediately.

May 3, 2017

Hi Long-Lost Mom :)

Your heart is amazing and it is so unfortunate that we didn't connect sooner. I did get your card a few days ago and I can say nothing... other than thank you for your heartfelt words... Wow :)

About coming to Vietnam, it is a great idea. If you want to bring one of the kids, preferably Paul (I speak to him more by far) or a friend is not a problem. I make all the schedules, and I can decide when I want to take time off. I can also help financially. The truth is, Vietnam is a great and safe place to travel.

The best is just fly here and we can take a couple of weeks to travel together if that is what you want. I think if you just come and see me for a day or two, you will be disappointed and leave unfulfilled. If you really want to come here before I go there... let me arrange things. :)

October can be done, but late February is best for me.

Big hugs :)

Trevor

Long-Lost Mom... The words went straight to my heart. I had struggled, wondering what to call myself and how to approach the subject of being his mother. I did not want to call myself Mom because I felt that title belonged to his real mom, the one who was by his side day in, day out. The one who taught him to speak, to walk, to share his toys. The one who woke in the night to care for him when he was not feeling well, consoled him and comforted him. She carried him in her arms and held him close to her heart, she supported him when he had difficult times. She was his real mom. I was the birth mother.

Yet I carried him during his first nine months, I felt his first kick and his first hiccups. My body nourished his. His cells were made from mine. I had given birth to him. I heard his first cry. How does one reconcile that?

Trevor later told me that he struggled with that question also because he wanted to be faithful to his mom whom he loved very much and at the same time be happy to have found me. Then one day, without thinking at all he sat down to write to me and the words just poured out: *Hi Long-Lost Mom.*

Yes, that is who I was. There was no comparison to be made, no right or wrong; it simply was. He had two moms. He honoured and loved both of us. One did not take away from the other; he was grateful for what each gave, and I realized I had permission to take my place in his life.

I also had permission to go to Vietnam to meet him. My mind was racing. It was all I needed to hear. In my excitement, I made a tentative plan to talk to the children about the idea. I wanted to start by discussing it with Paul since I had already made plans to visit with him and his family in June.

CHAPTER 11

Planning the Trip to Vietnam

June arrived quickly. Ideas, plans, and questions swirled around in my head. How would I break the news to Paul? Should I invite him and his wife to Vietnam, or just him? Would he want to come?

I was willing and felt quite capable of making the trip on my own because I had travelled frequently in the past seventeen years. The year 2000 had been my lucky year, and I finally graduated with a master's degree. After separating from my husband in 1980 and having a difficult time managing financially to support my three children, I came to the conclusion that education was the key. I had dreamt of studying at university since my last year in high school, however, I had taken a long detour when I became pregnant with Paul, followed by the pregnancy with Trevor, a ten-year marriage, and then a separation. At forty years old I'd been out of school for the past twenty-two years, so I was not confident that I would be successful.

I started by taking one class: Introduction to Psychology. I loved it! I had worked in hospitals in pediatrics and geriatrics as well as ran day-care centres and kindergartens, so learning about the development of children and the different stages one goes through in a lifetime wasn't new to me. Life had been my classroom; I simply needed to learn the vocabulary. To my surprise I did very well and was encouraged to continue. For the next twelve years, one class at a time, one course at a time, one semester at a time, I moved forward. Working part-time and sometimes full-time, my resumé grew as did my job opportunities and my salary. Finally, in the year 2000, with great pride, I donned a graduation gown. That was the year I landed my dream job and started travelling. From then on, I visited many countries in Europe along with Japan and China. I felt quite confident about going to Vietnam, and I was so anxious to talk to Paul about it.

While packing my suitcase for my trip to see Paul, I carefully made my plan. I decided to wait until Paul and my daughter-in-law were alone to explain the options. A whole year had gone by since Trevor first contacted me and I revealed my secret to Paul and his wife. Here I was, heading out for my yearly visit and once again there was big news to announce.

The flight landed on time, and my daughter-in-law greeted me at the airport. Her brother was on the same flight. After a warm hello and hugs, she said, "Paul couldn't come to welcome you because it is a very busy week for him and he will be working long hours."

"Oh, that's too bad. Has he already left for work?"

"No, he is at home anxiously waiting for you to arrive to say a quick hello. He will have time for a coffee with you before leaving. I will drop you off first so you can visit with him while I drive my brother to my mom's. I will be back at the house shortly."

Paul greeted me at the door. It is always so heartwarming to finally feel his arms around me for a strong but gentle hug after being far from him for months at a time. When we finally get together, we have so much to talk about. On that day, there was very little small talk. Due to my excitement, we had only been catching up for a few minutes when I blurted it all out.

"Guess what! I have decided to go to Vietnam to meet Trevor. Last year when I told you that he found me, one of your spontaneous responses to the news was that we should go meet him. Well, I wasn't ready at the time but I am now. I was thinking of going by myself, taking a cruise, and maybe getting to see him for a day or two. Then I had a better idea. If someone came with me, we could fly there and stay awhile. I could see where he lives and works and maybe visit Vietnam. I would like you to come with me."

"Wow! Oh, Mom, that is great!" Paul exclaimed, staring at me in astonishment.

"I meant to discuss this with the two of you in a calm, relaxing environment. I'm so excited about my decision to make the trip."

I can't recall his exact words, but something in his body language and his reply led me to believe the trip sounded exciting for him also. The only words I clearly remember were his assurances that he would love to go with me. I also remember some hesitation and caution about the affordability and responsibilities at work and with family plans. We agreed to let the information settle and we would discuss it later.

The front door opened and in walked my daughter-in-law.

"Have you two had time for a little chat?" she asked cheerfully.

"Yeeeees," he answered.

It was a slow motion yes which made me wonder if he was going to divulge the information or remain silent.

"Mom is going to Vietnam to meet Trevor and has asked me to go with her!"

I anxiously waited for her reaction. She understood the importance of the trip, and with her hand on her heart, she said they would do everything possible to see how they could make it happen.

Throughout the week, we discussed how we could make the trip a reality, and it looked like it might work. I let Trevor know that Paul was happy about the possibility of making the trip and meeting him. Paul and Trevor also exchanged emails where Trevor made suggestions about renting a beach house and swimming with whale sharks. Paul thought that would be awesome... I didn't!

Once home, I began to research Vietnam and flights. How would we get there? What was the shortest route? I would be leaving from Florida and Paul from Canada, so where would we meet up? How much would this all cost us? These were concrete questions which could be answered fairly quickly with a bit of research. The greatest questions remained a mystery. Was this really happening? How would I feel when I met him?

It seemed totally unimaginable that I would be travelling with "my two boys." I was very excited about it but still felt somewhat timid and uncomfortable about admitting out loud that I had two boys. Forty-six years of silence cannot be wiped away in one year. The fear of judgement, of reprimand, and of showing up exactly as who you are remains. Having the privilege of saying I have two sons was a blessing, yet it would take some getting used to. It would take courage to share my plans with friends and family. This was not just a physical trip I was planning; it was an emotional one for me and for the boys. None of us dreamt this could happen. As I let my imagination construct images of Paul, Trevor, and me exploring Vietnam, the trip was beginning to look more and more like a family vacation. I could feel the joy bubbling up inside me.

Memories of past vacations began to filter through my mind. After separating with my husband, family vacations became some of my happiest and most relaxing times. Money was scarce; however, I had managed to buy an old car and a tent trailer. Often on the very day school ended and summer holidays began, I would be waiting for the school bus to drive up the country road and let my children off at the driveway. The camper was stocked, hooked up to the car, and the gas tank was full. We had loaded all the canned goods, cereal, and non-perishables in the camper the night before. Of course, this included a box of sugar-coated cereal—the normally forbidden cereals—an expected camping treat. The picnic lunch was prepared. The children would help load their bags, toys, and games along with whatever fruit and vegetables were left in the fridge and we were on our merry way.

While I was married, we lived in Dalhousie, in northern New Brunswick, which was almost three hundred kilometres away.

We had left many friends there, and they were always eagerly waiting for us to arrive. I often left home with only fifty dollars in my wallet—twenty for gas on the way up, twenty for the return trip and ten left to spend. Before hitting the road, we made a customary stop at Grandma's house.

"You must stop to see me when you leave," she would remind me, "so I can give the children some spending money."

She would carefully place a five-dollar bill in each child's hand and lean over for a big hug. She often handed me a bag of fresh vegetables and berries from the garden.

As I remember it, the children got along so much better on vacation. Once the argument about who would be the first to sit in the front seat was over, they settled down with comic books or invented games such as who could count the most cars of a certain colour or spot the first cow or horse in the fields. Vacations brought a feeling of ease; of laughter and happiness. The anticipation of seeing our friends again and spending hours at the beach or at a friend's farm created an atmosphere of lightheartedness. There were no car seats and no air conditioning in the cars back then, so occasionally there would be disagreement about opening windows. We brought along a thermos of homemade lemonade as there was no bottled water in those days. I would hand out wet face cloths from a plastic bag to cool the children off.

Our favourite campground was free; it was a friend's backyard. She lived on a beach lot next to a playground. There was also a swimming pool close by where Paul and Danielle previously took swimming lessons. That was out of the question now because of lack of money, but they often walked over and watched, standing at the gate while instructors shouted out directives.

I remember one such day when Danielle came running back to the camper.

"Mom, where is my bathing suit? The instructor said we could go in for the swimming lesson!"

Fearing Danielle was in for a big disappointment, I walked to the pool to explain that I had not paid their subscription this year. The instructor informed me that the children's swimming lessons had been paid for the duration of our stay by a woman whom I did not even know. I got the bathing suits!

Along with my memories of past vacations and the excitement of soon travelling with my two sons, I realized I had not extended the invitation to my daughters. I assumed Natalie did not have any vacation time left and Danielle would probably have to take unpaid time off. Did they want to come? I hadn't even asked. I wrote to let them know we were in the process of planning a trip to meet Trevor, and Paul would most likely accompany me. I was so sorry I did not think of asking sooner if they were interested. Natalie said she wanted to come and could probably get the time off. It was more difficult for Danielle to organize two weeks off, but after explaining the circumstances to her employer, she was granted the time. I was more than thrilled. Could this really be possible? We would have an unimaginable family vacation! I shared the news with Paul and Trevor and both said it sounded great. During the following months the girls came home for a short summer vacation and we talked about making concrete plans. Secretly, I had hopes of having a family photograph taken with my four children.

It was quite a challenge to co-ordinate travel arrangements for four people leaving from three different cities. I was doing most of it and going back and forth between the children. A difficult aspect was finding suitable travel dates because four out of five needed to take time away from work. We chose the last two weeks of February as it seemed to be the best time for Paul. However, Trevor advised against it as it was the dates for the Tet holiday. During the celebration of the Vietnamese New Year, there are traditionally thousands of visitors. Hotels are booked solid, many things are closed, and most things are more expensive. The dates were changed several times to accommodate work engagements as well.

Once an agreement had been reached about dates, I began researching accommodations. The exchange rate was very favourable to the Canadian dollar, so we could afford four- and five-star hotels. We booked our first few nights at the Hilton, and I confirmed everything with Trevor. Next came choosing activities. Trevor wondered if there was something we wanted to see or visit, so I said we preferred the countryside to cities, and we loved water and walking on beaches. My priority was to spend time with him in his environment; this would be the number one thing on the list. The only other thing I really wanted to do was a cruise on Ha Long Bay. He agreed to book it and join us.

In the midst of me bombarding Trevor with information about airplane tickets, requesting information on places to stay, interesting things to do and visit, and best routes to travel, he was having his own challenges co-ordinating our visit at a very busy time in his life where they were expanding and relocating their business. Not wanting me to worry, he mentioned only a few times that he was very busy travelling from one location to another, however, he was putting an agenda together and all would fall into place. One of his emails was quite funny. It was September, and my daughters wanted to book our flights. I was writing back and forth with him trying to confirm arrivals and departure when I suddenly got this message: "OMG!!! You are not going to the moon. Stop worrying so much. Anytime is fine, just not the last two weeks of February. This is not rocket science." He had inserted smiling faces, and it made me laugh. It was immediately followed by an apology hoping that he didn't sound too arrogant; he just didn't want me to worry. It probably would be easier getting to the moon, I responded. We finally bought the tickets soon after.

In October 2017, news of the upcoming Winter Olympics in Pyeongchang, South Korea, was making headlines and there were concerns about the security at the airport in Seoul. We were scheduled to take a connecting flight in Seoul, so we were all somewhat worried. I asked Danielle and Natalie, who had taken charge of booking tickets, to please change our route. They soon confirmed that we would now be transferring in Hong Kong. While talking on the phone with Paul that day, he said he had to opt out of the trip because of work and family responsibilities. He regretted disappointing us but really felt he could not make the trip at this time. I was truly saddened but reassured him that he would be missed and I understood that he was the only one who knew what was best for him.

That evening I was leaving to facilitate another session. Paul had advised his siblings of his decision. It was understandable but disappointing to all, much more so I believed, to Trevor who had hopes of meeting his brother. Upon my return Sunday evening, I received an email from him.

September 29, 2017

Hi Yolande,

I hope all is well with you. I heard the bad news from Paul… very unfortunate. I have been thinking for some time now, regardless of Paul's decision. This is ridiculous…

I want to meet you with all my heart, I truly do, but coming to Vietnam with your family is simply crazy.

I understand for you and me, I really do, but for the rest… a trip to Vietnam? I am not sure they have an interest in meeting me. Face it, Yolande. It makes no sense for all of you to come here and waste all that money. That is just the way it is. Please don't make this harder than it has to be.

Cancel it all, and I will meet you where we will enjoy it the most… on the beach eating lobster together. :)

That is what this is all about.

Love always, your long-lost son,
Trevor

My heart sank. I wanted so much to take this trip and did not want to cancel it, so I immediately wrote to Trevor asking for some time to think it over.

October 2, 2017

Dear Trevor,

Sorry I did not answer sooner. I just came out of the cottage where I was giving a session. I had no access to Wi-Fi so I just read your message this afternoon. Paul has also told me of his decision. I am sorry to hear all this. Like you, I know one thing for sure; and that is I feel I love you already and I do want to meet you and see you in person. I do hear your concerns. Please give me some time to digest all this information, and I will get back to you in a few days once the turbulence settles down inside me so that I can make a clear decision.

I have confidence that we will meet and all will be well.

Sending love,
Your Long-Lost Mom♥

Now I was in crisis. It felt like my hope of being with Trevor would be gone once again. I became aware that my reaction was very intense and most likely it was not just because of what was happening today. The situation was reviving an old hurt just like when I was pregnant with him and hoped I could keep him and we could be a happy family. Again, without being conscious of it, I had dreamt of a pretend happy family just like I had done in my twenties. This time was different. I was not helpless. It was important that I at least express my feelings to Trevor and try to salvage the plan to go visit him. I gathered my thoughts and my courage and wrote him back.

October 6, 2017

Dear Trevor,

I think buying those tickets really shook all of us up because all of a sudden, all our hopes and fears became a reality. Sometimes, I agree with you that this is ridiculous and crazy, and I also have fears. But when I made the decision and agreed to be in contact with you about a year and a half ago when the social worker got in touch with me, I made that decision with the intention that saying yes to this journey of getting to know you would be good for all of us. It would be good for me, for you, and for my other three children. Now that does not mean that everything will be perfect and that we will all be a big happy family. It means that, starting with me, I will acknowledge and accept that what is, is. For me, it also means that I will do my best to help all my children, all four of you, to deal with the reality of what is.

One of my greatest fears throughout my life was that I would die without any of you knowing about each other and that you would all be left to deal with this alone after I am gone. I believe this is an opportunity for all of us to grow and simply accept one another just as we are. Yes, there will be family dynamics, and yes, we are all worried about how we will be accepted or if we will be accepted at all, but let's give it a try. What will be, will be. Trying to create a relationship on email is very difficult. And I am not getting any younger; if I want to make the trip it needs to be sooner than later. It is important for me to see you in your surroundings and see what you have created. It's all part of who you are. And the girls, Danielle and Natalie, are simply making that easier for me. They know how important this is to me and are doing their best to help make it happen.

This morning I decided to re-read all our emails to try to make sense of how this trip thing all started. It was back in January when you said that you would not be able to make it to Canada this year, and I asked you if I came to Vietnam, would you allow me to see you. You said yes. Then I started looking for ways to make it happen. First, I had thought of a cruise. It was you who suggested that only meeting for a couple of days would not be enough, and I agreed, but I thought it would be better than nothing. Then there was the possibility of going with Paul. Paul also thought the cruise was not the best idea because it was too expensive and we could fly there much cheaper. I knew Paul wanted to meet you and having a trip there with him would be a wonderful opportunity. Then I started doing research on Vietnam and discovered it would be a wonderful place to visit, and as we shared ideas it started feeling like a family vacation.

Then me being the mom, I remembered I had not even asked Danielle and Natalie if they would like to come. Here I was taking a trip with my boys and not even asking them if they wanted to join us. I really should have asked you first if it was OK with you. I got carried away with the thought of a family vacation. In my whole life, I would not even have dreamed this was possible. I was even hoping to get a family photo with all of us together. Maybe that will still happen some day! I hope so.

Anyhow, getting to your last email about let's cancel it all. I do not want to cancel it, Trevor. For whatever reason, I want to meet you sooner than later. We are all disappointed that Paul will not be with us. Danielle and Natalie do not want to cancel either and will try to change our route home this weekend so that we do not stop in Seoul. We can change some plans, though, if you would be more comfortable with it. It doesn't have to cost a fortune, and we do not need to spend a lot of money and to go all over the place. We can all pay our own way. The number one goal is for you and me to meet. The rest is just a bonus, and the girls will give us a lot of time alone; they have already told me that.

There are two things that would make me cancel this trip:

1. If you say that it is not safe for us to go.
2. If you feel you are not ready yet to meet me/us, then I will respect that.

Love you ♥

Trevor understood. After receiving word from him telling me not to stress over this, I let him know that we had purchased the new tickets. In order to cut expenses, the trip would be a little shorter and we would not include a visit to South Vietnam. The important thing was to spend time with him.

In December, along with Christmas wishes, Trevor sent a tentative agenda, and we confirmed the cruise on Ha Long Bay. Unfortunately, I was not able to get the dates we previously agreed upon as choices were limited. This time it was Trevor who opted out because he was moving the learning centre to another location on that day.

The anticipation was building. At times I felt like I was holding my breath just waiting for that day to arrive. It had been one year and eight months since I received that first letter from the social worker, and so much had changed. I was no longer afraid to meet him. I felt that all would go well although it was difficult to imagine actually meeting him.

Once, a long time before Trevor found me, I had been sitting in a garage while having my car repaired. There was a show on the television in the waiting room that focused on a mother being reunited with her long-lost son—it could have been *The Oprah Winfrey Show*. There was a lot of crying. I couldn't cope with the pain and became very emotional, so I left the room and only came back to retrieve my car a few hours later. I ran from it, never watching such shows and never reading about these kinds of situations. When talking with my daughters about meeting Trevor, I would admit that I had no idea how it might go, but I felt it would be fine. There was one thing I didn't want: drama. I heard myself say that many times. *No drama. I want no drama.* My plan was to get to the hotel and have a good night's sleep before meeting him so I would not fall apart when I saw him. I couldn't picture myself getting off the plane after a long flight and seeing him for the first time in the airport... too dramatic.

On the last day of December 2017, I checked in with Trevor.

> *Hi Trevor,*
> *In a month from now we will be together in Vietnam. Are you nervous yet? I am a little bit, but I am so looking forward to meeting you.*
>
> *Dear Long-lost mother,*
>
> *I am very much looking forward to meeting you. I have dreamed of this for a long time. I do wish it was in a different place and under different circumstances. The food is different here and the rooms are cold. I hope you will be okay. The time spent together will be great.*
>
> *Love Trevor*

We made the final plans in January.

> *Hi again,*
>
> *I just wanted to let you know, in case you are planning your time off from work, that you do not have to pick us up at the airport on Saturday because I reserved an airport transfer to the hotel in Hanoi. We will then have a good sleep and be ready to meet you on Sunday. You can pick the time and place. You know,*

Trevor, I was just wondering, since we have been waiting for this meeting for a long time, how would you like it to happen? Would you like to meet me alone or do you care if the girls are around? Will you come to the hotel? How is all this going to happen? Do you have any ideas/preferences? It is getting pretty exciting; in three weeks, we will meet in person!

In the meantime,
Sending hugs♣♥

Hi Yolande :)

Good question… I think I will come on Sunday afternoon after lunch since you will already be there and well-rested. Maybe it is best to meet you first and we can go for a walk by the lake. Then we can have dinner with the daughters. I don't think this trip has the same meaning for them, and we can get to know each other starting at dinner time at my friend's restaurant. What do you think…?

Love Trevor :)

I was so happy with his answer! Everything was falling into place! As I crossed the days off the calendar, we kept in touch.

January 15, 2018

Hi Trevor,
Just a few words to say that I am thinking about you. Calendar time says I will see you in a couple of weeks. As the time draws closer, I think of you often. I try not to imagine how it will be to actually see you

in person because I know that I could never imagine who you really are. I guess I will have to wait to live the experience and enjoy the moment! It is all getting pretty exciting!

Hope all is well with you.
Yolande ♣❤

January 16, 2018

Dear Yolande,
I am excited, too, and imagine meeting you will be incredible. A missing link from our lives :)

I look forward to taking many walks with you and knowing you better. I know it will be great to spend time with you and hear your stories.

All is as it should be, and all is well.

Love Trevor

January 24, 2018

Wow! Hard to believe this is really going to happen. Tomorrow I pack my suitcase, Thursday, I leave for Toronto to meet with Danielle and Natalie. Friday morning, we take the flight to Hong Kong— long flight—and then on to Hanoi! Saturday night I sleep, and Sunday I meet you!

See you soon,
Love,
Yolande

He soon replied…

> *Yes, Sunday we will finally meet in North Vietnam…*
> *Wow!!! It is amazing and unbelievable all together.*
> *I am running around in all three cities trying to get*
> *everything done so I can be free at this time. Wow!!!*
> *It's the only word I can use!*
>
> *Sunday we will walk… And all will be fine.*
>
> *Love,*
>
> *Trevor*

Not only did this seem unbelievable, there were days when it had been totally inconceivable. Looking back to the day when Trevor was born—April 20, 1970—I never thought I would ever see him again. With the help of people who surrounded me, mainly my cousin Georgie and her husband Louis, their four children and my little son Paul, I received enough life energy to maintain my sanity and stay alive. I was kept warm and fed. I found comfort from being around children.

There was another person who helped me keep my courage up. Not long after Paul and I moved into my cousin's home, an old friend whom I had met while working at the Children's Hospital School wrote to me. He had been in a serious car accident, suffered multiple broken bones, and spent months in hospital in a full body cast. He was now able to walk again using a cane.

"I have heard about what has happened to you," he said in his first letter. "I am wondering, could I come to see you?"

I wrote back thanking him for his concern but stating firmly that I was in no shape or mindset to see anyone at the moment. He inquired about Paul, so I let him know he was doing very well and would be a year old soon. He had developed the sweetest little personality; he was now walking and enjoying spending time playing with his little cousins. One letter led to another and my friend told me about his accident and what he had been through. Finally, he talked me into letting him drop in for a visit on Paul's birthday.

When he walked through that door, I forgot about my shame and embarrassment. I saw a young man who also had been broken by events in his life. Neither one of us were the same carefree young adults of a few years back. There was a seriousness about our stories that caused us to forge an immediate bond. The suffering had dug deep trenches in our hearts, and we could choose to fill these with kindness and understanding. Every following weekend that winter, he hitchhiked over three hundred kilometres to spend the weekends with Paul and me. At that time, my self-esteem was at its lowest. In his eyes though, I was still beautiful and worthy; I was still a good person. He said he had always loved me at a distance and now he could tell me. His courage gave me courage. Having a boyfriend visit me every weekend gave me hope. His visits gave me something to look forward to.

He was with me on that Sunday night when I began feeling like I was going into labour. He didn't want to leave, but he needed to be in class the following morning. It was that morning, in the early hours, that Trevor was born. With a sorrowful heart, I had to face the next moments. The only way I knew how to survive was to be strong; in all my weakness, I had to be strong.

After giving birth, I was wheeled into a room in which there were three other patients. I went through the motions of the stay at the hospital, spoke when I was spoken to, followed instructions. I cried and I slept and I willed myself to overcome. With another little one at home whom I loved dearly, I wanted to survive. I existed one hour at a time, one minute at a time, sometimes even one second at a time.

A few weeks after Trevor was born; my friend showed up with a diamond ring, and we were married that summer. I regained my place in society and in the eyes of the world of that time; I now had the right to be a mother. He adopted Paul and became his legal father. How cruel and blind a society can be to call any child illegitimate! Each new life is vibrant and has the right to be simply for being alive.

Our marriage blessed us with two beautiful and healthy daughters. Danielle came first: a blonde-haired, blue-eyed bundle of joy. She was quiet, reserved, creative, affectionate, and determined. At one and a half, she could be heard saying "a alone," her way of saying she could do things "all alone." On rainy days she could amuse herself for hours creating patterns and designs with toothpicks or a handful of hangers. When she played outside, she rarely needed toys; she found plenty of interesting things in nature. Flowers, sticks and stones, the sandbox, butterflies and little bugs were all fascinating. One day while helping her father weed the garden, she gently placed an earthworm on his shoulder.

"Look at the cute little wormy, Daddy!"

I saw his eyes widen as he tried to hide his surprise and gently remove the worm while agreeing with Danielle that it was indeed a cute little worm.

Four years later came Natalie; brown hair and big brown eyes, capturing everyone's hearts. Natalie was expressive, energetic, inquisitive, joyful, and loving. She spoke very early in life, and her favourite question was, "What that? What that, Mommy?"

"You know what that is, Natalie, it's a puppy," I would invariably respond.

Her reply always made people laugh. "Oh, 'cues (excuse me), me not think!"

Natalie loved the water and loved swimming. When she was four years old, she broke her collarbone while jumping on a mattress with friends. A few days later at the pool when I told her she could not swim because she was wearing a brace, she insisted she could swim anyhow. In the pool we went and she proved me wrong. She could swim under water with one good arm!

Who could have ever imagined that almost forty-eight years later I would be preparing to leave for Vietnam with my two lovely daughters to meet my long-lost son?

CHAPTER 12

Trip to Asia

Arriving at the Toronto airport at 4:00 p.m. on a weekday was not a great idea. As I followed the long corridors to find a taxi to take me downtown, I was told that the wait time was an hour and a half to two hours. The man at the gate suggested that I take the Go Train to Union Station. It would only take a half hour, and from there I could catch a cab. What he didn't tell me was that people were lined up, some aggressively pushing their way into the first cab that made a stop at Union Station. A very nice young man whom I had just met stood with me while we waited our turn. The snow was gently falling, and the weather was cool but mild. Slush was accumulating, soon deeper than my sneakers. My new-found acquaintance suggested that we walk a bit down the street to hail a cab before it reached the crowd, and he helped with my suitcase. His idea worked. About a block and a half later, we happily hopped into a cab. The cab driver laughed as we told him our story, and I gave him the address of my hotel. Had we walked another few blocks we would have been at the front door.

My heart raced as I checked into my hotel room. I was the first one to arrive. In my room I settled in, unpacking very little as we would be there less than twelve hours. I called my granddaughter. Maeve is Paul's oldest daughter who lives and works in Toronto.

"Mémére!" she exclaimed. "Where are you?"

"At the Best Western close to the airport. Room 203. I am so excited to see you. How long will it take for you to get here?"

"About one hour depending on traffic. I will hurry. See you soon!"

Meanwhile, after a full day at work, Danielle and Natalie rushed to catch the first evening flight to Toronto. The weather had been accommodating and we were relieved, given that in Canada a snowstorm at any one of the airports could have caused us to be on different flights. I received a message from Danielle saying they were about to board. Excitement filled the air as Maeve entered the room. She is always so expressive.

"Sorry I took so long. I was having trouble with my cat."

"That's okay dear, I'm just happy to see you. Come sit with me and tell me all about what is happening in your life."

We cozied up on the sofa and caught up on the latest events. Soon there was a knock on the door and another wave of excitement as the girls arrived. By now, I was absolutely starving. I like eating early, and it was already late for me.

"Enough of this catching up, you ladies. I am hungry. Let's go eat!"

"Get used to it, Mom," one of the girls laughed. "Your meal routine is about to change greatly for the next two weeks!"

How true! I thought. This trip was not only going to change my meal routine, it was about to change my life!

After dinner, conversations continued to flow freely as the three of them sat on the bed in the hotel room recalling other times we have been together, catching up on the new adventures in their lives, on their hopes and dreams. I sat across from them, appreciating the moment, enjoying their company, and taking a few snapshots to freeze the memory.

One of the things we talked about was Trevor finding me and how excited I was to be making this trip to meet him. Maeve had many questions. She wondered if I had done any research about reunions of estranged family members and what to expect.

"No," I answered. "I never watch or read about reunions; it would make me upset. I don't want it to be a big thing, although I know it is a big thing. I don't want any drama around the meeting. No photos, no videos. I just want to live the moment. It will be captured in my heart. I want it to be peaceful so I can savour it. I have no idea how it will go. I just know I want to do this. It will be what it will be, and I feel it will all work out."

The evening did not have enough hours to contain all the sharing. At one o'clock in the morning, I found myself apologising for suggesting that it was time to get some sleep and break up the party.

Five hours later, my adrenaline from the anticipation along with a cup of coffee provided me the energy needed to get to the airport. Our boarding passes had already been printed so we went directly to security. All went well.

After finding our gate it was time for one of my favourite things: breakfast! We found a Starbucks for Natalie's coffee. I picked up some fruit and reserved a table while the girls stood in line to get coffee, tea, and chocolate croissants! Our first flight was non-stop Toronto to Hong Kong.

I had visited Hong Kong once before when a travel agency offered great prices to travel from Quebec to China for the 2010 Expo in Shanghai. A friend and I took advantage and joined a group for a very memorable three-week tour of China, which ended in Hong Kong. Once the girls and I boarded and were settled in our seats for the long flight, I told them a few stories of my visit in Hong Kong. The first thing that came to mind was how many of us Canadians felt disoriented when the cars drove on the left side of the road, like they do in England. Another memory was of a man washing the windows of a glass dome on top of a very tall building without any harness or safety gear whatsoever. In Hong Kong, as in many parts of China, there seemed to be very few safety rules. The adventure which stood out the most was when the group stayed in a luxurious hotel, possibly one of the most impressive places I've ever stayed, on the final night of the tour. I don't recall if I was on the sixty-fourth or the sixty-ninth floor, but I know I was in a skyscraper tall enough to make the other towering buildings look miniature. The room was shaped in a semicircle, and windows from floor to ceiling covered the whole surface. As darkness fell, the blue-grey sky got darker and the clouds seemed almost black. The sun going down behind them broke through casting rays of orange, yellow, and flickering silver light on the Bay of China. Boats seemed to be gliding in slow motion on the clear and calm surface of the water. The awesome image was forever imprinted in my mind. However, that was not the point of the story. As I entered the room, I noticed a set of gas masks on a shelf. The instructions read: "PLACE ON FACE. WALK DOWN STAIRS. DO NOT USE ELEVATORS!"

At 2:00 a.m., the fire alarm went off! I did not want to leave my room! I opened the door leading to the hall at the same time as a man in the next room opened his. He was in his shorts and me in my nightdress, and we stared at each other, speechless for a moment.

"What do we do?" I asked.

A lady ran down the hall saying something in Chinese that we couldn't understand.

"Maybe call downstairs?" he suggested.

I made the call.

"False alarm, please sleep now," the lady at the reception told me.

Easy to say, more difficult to do!

On the flight, we were fed a few meals, watched movies, and wondered what Vietnam would be like. At one point, we became giddy and laughed over nothing just from being so tired that the least little thing became hilarious. We finally managed to sleep for a few hours. Often, I would just close my eyes to enjoy the present moment.

When we finally disembarked in Hong Kong, we were very tired—the kind of tiredness one feels when you are sleepy but can't sleep, when you are hungry but can't eat, and when some moments feel real while others are surreal. It was as if we were in a dream. Relieved to set foot on solid ground after more than fifteen hours of flying, passengers filed out of the airplane and into the busy airport. It felt good to walk around, stretch our legs, and realize we were now in Asia.

Once the crowd dissipated, the airport seemed quite spacious. The fog in the distance, moving onto a large body of water, shielded distant islands and fading mountains. At the edge of the water, where one might expect to see a sandy beach, planes were landing and leaving the runway which ran parallel to the water. Right below us numerous aircraft were stationary while some were arriving and others departing the gates. We would be boarding our next flight to Vietnam at one of these gates at 5:30 p.m., which was 5:30 a.m. our time.

Darkness was falling when the plane landed in Hanoi on that night of January 27, 2018. It had been a long trip; three flights and almost thirty-six hours to reach our destination. Hundreds of people who seemingly knew where they were going marched to the carousels to find their luggage, so we followed. Standing in line at customs, staring at all the signs written in Vietnamese, we questioned whether we should move ahead individually or as a group. It was evident that we were foreigners. It was our turn to be the minority. I remember thinking how frightening it must be for refugees entering a new country. We observed that everyone approached the customs officer one by one, even children, unless they were very young, so we did the same. Once through customs, we made our way to the exit. I had reserved a shuttle to drive us into the city. Amidst the large crowd, we somehow managed to find our driver, a middle-aged Vietnamese man, holding a sign with our names. We followed him to the car. The night air was cool and a slight drizzle was falling, making everything feel damp. Our driver did not speak English, but he nodded as we told him the name of our hotel. Once we left the airport, we drove for almost an hour, and the sky grew quite dark. The traffic was moderate and there was a lot of honking. Each time we passed a vehicle or were passed by another we heard the *honk, honk, honk.* I strained my eyes looking out at the scooters that seemingly appeared out of nowhere, some without a single light, zig-zagging through in the very dark night.

As we approached the city, the traffic grew heavier and slower. Narrow houses, two or three stories high, along with small businesses which were not very well lit, were crowded together. The rain fell heavier now, and the commotion intensified the deeper we drove into the city. Thousands of men, women, and children lined the streets. There was definitely something going on and it was very festive. The honking of the horns was loud and constant. Some buses with people hanging out of the windows and blowing party horns joined the cacophony. It was clear that something was being celebrated, but we had no idea what.

"Wonder what's going on," I said to the girls. "Do you suppose they are already celebrating the Tet holiday?"

We laughed nervously as we watched in disbelief. The crowds and the police were on every corner. Our driver deftly dodged pedestrians, scooters, cars, and buses. A policeman signalled to him that the road was closed and indicated that he should keep driving. He continued on to the next road, and again rolled the window down, exchanged a few words, and the officer pointed to keep going. Once again, the driver tried another street with the same results. Finally, he started backing up slowly onto the sidewalk. By now I was scared. There were hundreds of people on the sidewalk.

"Oh my God! What is he doing?" I exclaimed.

He confidently and slowly honked his way onto the sidewalk and turned off the engine. Then he turned to us and waved his hand indicating that we were to follow him. With a wiggle of his index and middle fingers, we understood we were going to walk. He unloaded our suitcases, grabbed two of them, and pushed his way through the crowds.

"Mom, hang on to the suitcase and don't lose him, we are right behind you!" one of the girls said.

I had to laugh because otherwise I would've cried.

"This is crazy!" I said, half running to keep up with him.

Fortunately, we didn't have to go too far, perhaps a block or two, until we spotted our hotel. He was kind enough to walk us right into the hotel to make sure we were safe.

"Should we tip him?" Natalie asked.

"Yes, a big one!" Danielle and I answered at the same time.

We all laughed as he bowed, bidding us a goodnight in his own way.

At the desk, we asked about the celebrations and were told it was a party for the homecoming of the football team who had played against China.

"Well, congratulations on the win!" I said brightly.

"Oh, no," the hotel attendant replied, "we lost!"

As the door to our bedroom shut behind us, I sighed in relief.

"I never want to go back out there again!" I said, laughing and knowing full well I would be anxious to explore in the morning.

On Saturday, January 27, 2018, I wrote to Trevor to let him know we had arrived.

> *Hi Trevor!*
>
> *We are actually really in Hanoi! The trip was not too painful at all, but we are tired. Also, we had quite a joy ride from the airport to the hotel because there were parties in the streets, etc. At the desk we were told that it was because of the football game that was played today against China. We will tell you all about it tomorrow.*
>
> *So, tomorrow, do you have any idea around what time you will be coming? I have access to my email*

because I have my iPad. We are in room 341, so you can call the hotel or if we should be out for breakfast or lunch you can call Danielle's phone.

See you soon! ☺

Trevor responded…

Wow! You are really here. This is amazing :)

I am in Ha Long City now, and I will be heading up tomorrow morning at 9:30 a.m. so I should be there in three or four hours from then. Probably around 1 p.m.

I will go to the lobby and call you :)

It was not long before we fell into a long, deep sleep.

CHAPTER 13

Reunion

On Sunday, January 28, 2018, I opened my eyes and scanned the room. It had been difficult to find a hotel in Vietnam where three beds were allowed in one room. It was a large room with a sitting area, two single beds and an additional one added at my request. My daughters were still sleeping. My attention went to my heart. It was still beating, and I gave thanks for the realization that this was not a dream. I was really in Vietnam! Danielle, Natalie, and I had slept almost twelve hours straight, exhausted from our travels. Not wanting to disturb the girls, I very quietly reached for my iPad and silenced the ringer. I felt as if I was whispering as I wrote to Trevor.

> *Good morning Trevor,*
>
> *We had a great sleep and are just waking up now. Am really happy and excited, and surprisingly not feeling nervous. It just seems like the natural and wonderful thing to do! I will be waiting for your call!*

The reply came quickly, Trevor gave his phone number in case he had to be reached.

Good morning,

Yes, it is all natural, just took a long time coming :)
Leaving soon :)

Trevor

The girls soon woke up. We readied ourselves, and down we went to the dining room for breakfast. Most of the travellers in the quiet seating area were Asian. The layout was exquisite. Carved watermelons, giant grapefruits, green mandarins, and abundant fruit of various kinds and shapes adorned the tables. Danielle introduced me to fresh dragon fruit and passion fruit, which I had never tried before. We talked about our arrival in Hanoi the previous night, describing it as hilarious, nerve-racking, insane, funny, overwhelming, interesting, and scary to say the least. We tried to stifle our laughter, which caused a few curious glances to be cast our way. Later, strolling through the lobby, we discovered a bakery and gift shop. Strings of pearls and jewellery made from seashells caught my attention, as I was looking for something special for a friend who was about to celebrate her sixty-fifth birthday, but somehow, I could not concentrate on gift buying on this particular morning.

Once the girls made their purchases of a few sweet treats, we returned to our room to check emails and the weather forecast. I was a disappointed to find that it would be a cloudy day with showers. When Trevor and I had discussed how and where we would like to meet, he had mentioned there was a lake nearby where we could go for a walk. Rain or no rain, I was determined to have a great day. Through the window of our hotel room, I could see a lush garden. Flowers of every colour of the rainbow lined the sidewalks. Despite the drizzle, people were walking leisurely and a few were riding bicycles. It was twelve thirty, and Trevor was supposed to show up at one o'clock. Only another half hour to wait. A quick scan of my mind and body reassured me that I was feeling calm. There were no signs of panic, sadness, or fear.

While the girls answered their emails and chatted about what was going on back home, I leaned back in a large, comfortable blue armchair to relax and reflected on how anxious I had been eighteen months ago when the journey started. The fear of meeting Trevor in person had been the worst. That fear of falling apart was always present in my subconscious along with the need of being in control. Perhaps this is why, in preparing to come to Vietnam to meet Trevor, I kept insisting I wanted no drama, no photos, no people around, no tears, nothing which would cause me to become overly sensitive and fall apart. I scanned inside of myself again. There was no trace of that fear. Even if I still could not imagine stepping into that moment, I felt confident we would be all right.

"I think I'll go downstairs and surprise him," I told the girls as I sprang out of my chair.

"Do you want us to come with you?" one of them asked.

"No, I'm fine. I'd like to go alone. I'll let you know later what's going on."

Because I could not find the stairway, I took the elevator down to the second floor. From there I went down the grand staircase, which had an allure of royalty and brought to mind images of women in stunning gowns and men dressed to perfection making an entrance. For an instant, I almost felt royal as I walked down the stairs. There was, after all, a magical fairytale story going on that day. Hand on the railing, anchored in the present, I descended slowly and embraced this moment of worthiness and dignity. I had beaten myself down with self-shame for so long, but as I descended the staircase in that moment, I felt proud and worthy of my own respect.

The hotel lobby was large, with two main entrances, a bar, and some small shops. I strolled around for a few minutes, appreciating the art on the walls, admiring the beautiful chandeliers, and observing people checking in and out at the front desk. I was doing my best to stay in the moment. I knew what Trevor looked like from the photos he had sent me, so I would not have difficulty recognizing him as there were not many Caucasians entering the hotel, let alone redheads!

I wandered slowly between the two main entrances, glancing through the window and looking for any sign of him in the parking lots. I was totally focused on finding him, waiting, breathing, and occasionally checking the clock. Five minutes went by, then ten. I was waiting for the hand of the clock to strike the exact second when my whole life would change, that exact second that marked before and after. My mind seemed to be in limbo, suspended in time, waiting in anticipation for the moment to reveal itself, for it was still impossible to imagine the next scene.

As the clock approached the fifteen-minute mark, I turned away from what I considered the rear parking lot door.

"Looking for someone?" a man asked.

I took a deep breath and held it. I knew I was hearing my son's voice for the first time. I turned to face him. There he stood! My eyes fell upon a tall, kind looking, red-haired man. His smile melted my heart.

"Oh my God! It's you!"

I reached out to him. The words *He's mine* resonated within me. He opened his arms and we embraced. He felt strong, yet the hug was gentle as he held me tenderly in a moment of stillness. I felt my heart relax as if chains had been broken. Stepping back slightly, still holding hands, we peered into each other's eyes, acknowledging one another's existence.

"I can't believe it's you! You're really here!"

"I just can't believe this is happening!"

In our hearts there was no doubt, only a deep knowing. *My baby! My mom!* We exploded into laughter as we stood there holding hands and gazing at each other. I wanted to surprise him, but while I was walking from door to door, he spotted me and snuck in through the back door. He was the one to surprise me!

Still holding my son's hands, I felt an electrical current running through me. Knowing I had a child whom I had left behind forty-six years ago and then seeing him in the flesh—actually holding his hands—were two totally different experiences. All these years there had been a large gap within me, my heart wanting to move towards my child, my mind guarding against the past and the pain. The battle was over. Heart and mind were going in the same direction. The search was finally over for Trevor as well.

"Would you like to sit down?" Trevor asked.

While walking around the lobby waiting for him, I had noticed a semi-circular, red leather sofa in a small alcove under the staircase. It seemed inviting and somewhat private.

"I would love to sit, and I know exactly where," I replied as I led him to the cozy corner. Our familiarity with each other was tangible. Something in his voice and mannerisms reminded me of Paul. The resemblance to my father was evident—his eyes, his smile, his red hair. It made my heart happy. I recognized in him a kindness which I have sometimes felt in myself. I have always thought it had been inherited from my dad. We sat close enough to touch; a hand, a shoulder, a knee. Smiling, eyes searching for answers. One question followed another, but neither one of us was in any state to really hear or absorb it.

"How was your trip?"

"Why are you living in Asia?"

"Where did you go after I was born?"

"How did you find me?"

Each question was followed by a quick answer and a promise to talk about it later, much laughter, and an occasional, "I can't believe I am actually seeing you!"

Once the adrenaline had settled, we began to calm down. Trevor pulled out a cigarette, apologised for being a smoker, and we began to plan our afternoon.

"Would you care to go for a walk? I think the rain has stopped. Perhaps, we could grab a bite to eat."

On our way out, he explained that a former girlfriend had recently come back into his life, and he would be picking her up later at the airport. She would be with us this evening. After letting the girls know I would be back later and that Trevor would be joining us for dinner around seven o'clock, we made our way to the lake.

Crossing the road in Hanoi can be a challenge. The traffic is often heavy with scooters, motorbikes, and trucks scrambling for their share of the road. I noticed that some motorists paid scant attention to the traffic lights, and as we stood at the corner waiting to cross, the traffic light changed. I hesitated.

"Don't hesitate," Trevor said, as he grabbed my hand and escorted me across a very busy intersection. "Just indicate that you are crossing and walk."

"Okay." I wasn't sure I liked that idea.

Note to self: If the girls and I must go somewhere alone, wait until there are many people crossing and stand in the middle of the crowd while they walk across the street.

On the main road, amongst the many traditional Vietnamese businesses and the majority of signs written in that language, something seemed out of place. The presence of North American companies was evident even in this faraway land. The temperature was cool and damp, perhaps 15°C, and I was happy to be wearing my windbreaker. Trevor had advised us to dress in layers because the temperature could average 17–22°C in North Vietnam. This was winter!

The surroundings became quieter as we approached the lake; there were a few street vendors and an entire street had been closed off to traffic. The majority of people out strolling were young adults and teens. Families with one or two children were out enjoying the afternoon. Two school-aged children rollerbladed past and many were on bicycles, all without helmets. Younger children in little go-carts squealed with delight as their parents looked on. There were signs of old and new traditions. Old statues of famous people or events, a mural of a tiger, small pagodas and altars honouring ancestors were reminders of ancient traditions. We saw very few elderly folks out walking. Teens with phones in hand and ear buds in their ears gathered around a wall that displayed hundreds of backpacks. It was a store, wide open, with no side walls, only one back wall with a few awnings above it to protect from the rain. Flowers grew everywhere. The peach and apricot trees were beginning to bloom.

As I breathed in the sweet scent of fresh flowers, most of which I could not identify, I became aware that I was mainly breathing in Trevor's presence. I hung on to his every word as he explained how he came to be adopted by his parents. They were childless and had been planning to move to the United States because his dad and a friend wanted to start a business there. His parents had planned to adopt a child once they settled. This was in the late sixties, during the Vietnam War. While filling out the legal paperwork, they learned that if they became American citizens, there was a possibility of being drafted. This was daunting. Americans were crossing the border into Canada at that time to avoid the draft. In the end, they decided to stay in Canada, buy a house, and adopt a child there. And so it was. The war in Vietnam had altered the course of his life. And now, paradoxically, it was in Vietnam that he had reunited with me, his birth mother.

"Why did you settle in Vietnam?"

"I am a dreamer and a traveller," he answered. "I had once seen pictures of this breathtaking scenery with the beautiful mountains jutting out of the bay, and I longed to see it. There was a certain moment in my life as a young adult, after studying a bit and trying different types of work, when I was deciding where I would like to live. I chose to come here."

While walking around the lake, I listened as he shared the parts of his journey that had led us to this day. Later, he walked me back to the hotel so I could rest and freshen up for dinner.

The girls were waiting, and I was eager to tell them about my afternoon.

"It went well!" I exclaimed. "I just can't believe it… there are just no words to describe how I feel… he is real… he looks like our family… there were no tears! We were just so happy to see each other!"

Short sentences were all I could muster, and I paused in between to feel each emotion, to remember the words we had spoken. How could I explain the excitement, the happiness? I felt overwhelmed and yet, deep down, there was a peace I had never experienced. Being able to share this with my girls multiplied my happiness. They were happy that the meeting had gone well. They knew how important it was for me.

They told me how they, too, had experienced crossing the busy road. They had taken care to cross in the middle of a group of people who seemed to know how to make it to the other side. Also, they had discovered the lake and walked the trail around it, but we had not seen each other.

After a short rest, it was time to get ready to go downstairs since Trevor was meeting us for dinner at seven o'clock. When the girls and I arrived at the lobby, he was waiting. As he stood and walked towards them, I noticed how much taller Trevor was. They smiled, hugged, and exchanged a few words. I treasured the moment. I looked on, affectionately wondering what was going on in their hearts and minds. I wished Paul could have been there, but that would be for another time and place. Trevor introduced his girlfriend and let us know she would be travelling with us. We then made our way up the grand staircase to the restaurant.

The hostess escorted us to our seats and handed out the menus, which turned out to be a great conversation starter. I felt a bit nervous and pondered whether anyone else might be feeling the same. The ambiance created by the decor and Asian music in the background gave a soothing Zen-like feeling. I was relieved to see the menus had an English translation. The waitresses, wearing traditional Vietnamese dresses, were happy to answer our questions as we discussed our meals. The conversation seemed to flow easily between the girls and Trevor as they spoke about the school they had attended and remembered some of the teachers. They moved on to their present-day lives and the work they were doing. The setting was perfect, but it was difficult to fully appreciate that first meal together. I was exhausted. Along with the jetlag, the emotions and excitement of the day had caught up with me. At home, it would have been seven o'clock in the morning. Despite the fatigue, we enjoyed a delicious meal and a pleasant evening. We made plans to meet the next morning and did not linger too long, knowing we would have plenty of time together later on. We also longed to fall into our beds!

On the way out of the restaurant, I caused a small commotion by tripping and stumbling on a flower planter. It was embarrassing, but I was not hurt. Perhaps I was more nervous than I thought!

CHAPTER 14

Together in Vietnam

There is an instant, as we awaken in the morning, when we tip into awareness and become conscious of our surroundings. When I awoke from my slumber on that second day in Hanoi, I knew my surroundings were not my usual ones, but I also quickly noticed that my interior landscape had also changed. There was an unusual lightness of heart, a sense of relief, and a feeling of being open to the experience. Thoughts travelled through my mind.

> *Wow! I'm still in Vietnam and my girls are with me.*
> *Wow! I met Trevor.*
> *Wow! Now what?*

Trevor had made an itinerary of how many days we would stay at each destination. My interior itinerary, on the other hand, was like a book with blank pages. I hadn't been able to imagine how I would feel standing in front of my son in real life, so I didn't think much beyond that point. Although I didn't know what would come next emotionally, I felt happy and was eager to see Trevor again.

"Ready to hit the road?" Trevor asked as he and his driver picked us up at the hotel. "Let's get these suitcases loaded in the van; we have a four-hour drive to Ha Long Bay. We will stop somewhere on our way out of Hanoi for a bite to eat. You absolutely have to try some Pho, a favourite dish in Vietnam."

Pho is a rice noodle soup with meat and various greens which Trevor and company were raving about. I thought it was good, but I was hesitant to eat the local food having been ill in China a few years back.

We drove through picturesque villages on our way to Ha Long Bay and enjoyed the unfamiliar landscape of the countryside. Rice paddies of numerous shades of green, farmers with conical hats working in their fields, and an occasional water buffalo all zipped by in the blink of an eye. From time to time one of us would try to freeze the memory with a snapshot. One thing which stood out for me was the small cemetery lots and burial tombs which dotted the endless rice patties. Trevor explained that, not so long ago, members of the family were buried in the fields where the crops grew.

The seating in a van does nothing to enhance conversation, so I was deep in thought during most of the trip. I remembered all the time and care that had been put into the planning of this trip as well as the worries that had flared up while researching and booking the hotels. The possibility had occurred to me that things could go wrong. I was going to a country I did not know to meet a man I did not know.

"What if he doesn't show up, Mom?" one of the girls had asked.

I did not worry about that situation because the thought never occurred to me. I had the advantage of getting to know Trevor from our correspondence, but I knew they were much savvier than I when it came to meeting people through the internet. If the situation were reversed and it was one of my girls leaving for such a trip, I would definitely be worried, so I took them seriously and felt safer having a plan "B." Even though Trevor had generously offered to take care of things, I chose to make most of the reservations myself. Yet, from the moment I met him I never feared for my safety. This is not to say I always felt safe driving in a van in Vietnam, but that is another story!

From time to time during the long drive, one of us would ask a question or make a comment which would spark a short conversation about the country or the customs, but the intriguing scenery mainly held our attention. I couldn't help thinking how the drive must have seemed endless for Trevor. He wanted to make sure his guests were comfortable and had invited one of us to take the front seat with the driver and the other two in the middle seat. This left Trevor, his girlfriend, and a few suitcases crammed in the rear seat. He is tall and a smoker, so I wondered how he was going to cope for four hours. Other than a few disagreements with the driver about which road to take, which restaurant we would stop at for Pho, and what type of music to play on the radio, all went well.

The scenery looked totally different as we approached the port city of Ha Long. Beyond the buildings, we could see the bay. Many small islands rose up from the water like mountain peaks. I was not familiar with the geography or topography of Vietnam, so I was curious about how deep this bay could be. I wondered if perhaps the mountains were like icebergs where the greater mass lies under the water. In doing some research while preparing the trip, I discovered that Ha Long Bay is a UNESCO World Heritage Site and is listed as one of the New 7 Wonders of Nature. It is also called Vinh Ha Long, which means "Where the dragon descends to the sea." With a bit of imagination, the mountain peaks did look like sea dragons.

I felt excited as we drove past a large modern amusement park, and I noticed a gigantic Ferris wheel. I had loved amusement parks in my youth, and the Bill Lynch Show were the words that came to mind. Trying to retrieve the memories, I momentarily slipped into the past. The Bill Lynch Show was the travelling carnival which brought rides, amusements, and games to the small town of Shediac every summer during the Lobster Festival. Shediac prides itself as being the Lobster Capital of the World and has been celebrating this event for the past seventy years. As I remembered it, the festivities brought families and neighbours together, and many who had moved away would return for a summer visit during the festival week. In my earliest memories, I see myself walking on the festival grounds holding my dad's hand and dodging the puddles after a refreshing summer shower which had sent the crowds seeking shelter under tents and awnings. The smell of the wet soil was soon overtaken by the scent of cotton candy and homemade fries. The bright swirling lights on the rides dimmed the stars which had reappeared after the clouds passed. The squeals and screams of young and older children pierced the silence of the night. It was a happy time. The memories brought a feeling of being carefree.

Trevor's voice brought me back to the present moment. We had arrived in a remarkable area of the city where new, imposing, all-white buildings lined both sides of the streets.

"Many old buildings were torn down to make room for these modern structures. Government is investing millions into tourism in this area. This will no doubt create jobs, along with a need for locals to learn to converse in English, so this is where the new learning centre will open. Come, I will give you a tour."

It was a four-storey building; the first three floors would house the learning centre, and the top floor was to be Trevor's apartment. His furniture was gathered in one room and covered with a canvas drop cloth as workers completed the kitchen area. From the balcony, there was a view of the water and a large cruise ship could be seen farther out in the bay. While the girls explored the school, Trevor and I lingered upstairs. His phone rang several times.

"I apologise for all these interruptions, but I'm afraid it will be like this most of the time during your visit."

"That is okay," I said.

"When we started planning your visit here, I knew big changes were coming with the businesses, but I had no idea it would all happen so fast. Remember I told you I was planning on taking over a small hotel and moving the restaurant there?"

"Yes, I remember I had asked if we could stay at your hotel, but you didn't think it would be ready. You also said it would mostly house your staff, the teachers who arrive from different countries to teach English," I said.

"There was no way of knowing it would all happen at the same time," he replied. "There is a race for the market here in Ha Long City."

"I can understand that. Last night, I laid awake for a while because I wasn't able to fall asleep. I replayed my day in my mind: meeting you, spending the afternoon together, our walk in the park, and dinner with the girls. I felt so grateful and fulfilled that I was ready to leave for home anytime. My mission was accomplished, I already felt full. So, all this is extra, it's a bonus. Please do not stress over this. I am really fine and totally happy. I love travelling. I will enjoy you when you can be with us, and the rest of the time I will take advantage of this wonderful trip with my girls."

Trevor paused, looked at the water in the distance, and sighed.

"I really want to spend as much time as I can with you," he said. "But right now, I need to take you to Cam Pha because I have to go to work for a few hours. You three can check into your hotel, relax, and have a little rest. I will join you this evening for a walk and dinner at my restaurant."

"Sounds good to me," I replied. "I still feel a little jet-lagged."

"Don't expect anything fancy. It is just a small place where we make homemade western-style food. Pizza is our specialty."

Cam Pha is a coal mining city and does not attract many tourists. The district stretches over 486 kilometres between mountain and sea and has approximately two hundred thousand inhabitants. There were rows upon rows of narrow three- or four-storey houses near our hotel that had a garage-like door on the first floor that rolled up to reveal small businesses. Each family sold anything from tea to clothes, flowers to hardware. Some of these garage-like areas served as gathering places where the men would sit on small stools and play cards, drink tea or beer, and smoke. Smoking is very popular in Vietnam. "No Smoking" signs are practically non-existent. The residents are mostly poor, and there is a lot of pollution. Trevor had said two days in Cam Pha would be enough because we were mainly there to visit the learning centre. The next day we met Ms. Le, whom Trevor had met several years before when she owned and ran a small learning centre in her home. They soon recognized that they had similar goals and visions for education which would meet the needs of children and adults in learning conversational English. Together they expanded the centre and opened a second one in nearby Van Don. As we entered, the staff seemed happy to see him. With his arm around my shoulder, he proudly introduced us to the staff.

"This is my mother Yolande, and my two sisters Danielle and Natalie. They came from very far to visit."

I don't know how much they knew about our story, but they eagerly welcomed us with broad smiles and spoke to us in English. The atmosphere felt relaxed as Trevor joked with his staff. A huge map of the world hung in one room, and Danielle showed a few of the staff members where we lived and had travelled from. On our way out, it was very touching to hear a chorus of young Vietnamese children singing a very popular North American children's song for us. With tiny hands on their hearts, they sang and gestured: "I love you." As we stepped out of the learning centre, Trevor suggested we head back to Ha Long.

"It's much nicer there with more things to see and do. I will have a leisurely coffee with you, and then I need to put in a few hours of work. Ms. Le and I will join you later for lunch. Is there anything in particular you would like to see or do today?"

"Trevor, today I need photos. I would like very much to have a photo of you and me."

"Well, that can be easily arranged providing you promise to share them. I will take you ladies to the waterfront where the scenery is amazing, and we will take all the photos you would like."

Back in Ha Long, once the girls and Trevor had their coffee and I my *green* tea—much to my dismay for it is practically impossible to get hot black tea in Vietnam—Trevor lingered for a while and made sure I got photos of him and me alone as well as photos of all four of us. I was thrilled! Imagine something that you believe to be impossible actually happening. I would have a photo of myself with my son Trevor to take home with me!

I developed a passion for photography many years before when I was desperately searching for photos of my dad. Photos were rare in those days, and it was a treasure to find even a few to remember those who came before us. Sometimes it is all you have to remember a person, stir a memory, or soothe a longing. Dad owned a Kodak Brownie, a little black box in which a film was carefully placed. It would usually take twelve shots, half of which were often blurred or ruined if you clicked twice without winding the film. I was fascinated with that camera and the many cameras I have purchased since.

We told Trevor about the numerous albums which I kept at home that documented my children's lives. I sighed as I remembered having hoped for a photo of myself with all my children. I was sorry Paul would not be in this first picture with him.

Trevor left for work, and the girls and I decided to go for a walk and perhaps do a bit of shopping. Walking along the bay, we saw the stunning contrast between the old and new ways of life. The scenery to our right was peaceful. Hundreds of fishing boats, some small, some large, many of which housed families, rested on the still water. We took many photos as we tried to imagine how different this life must be. Some had laundry hung on clotheslines strung across the boat. Behind them, mountains peeked out of the water and served as a backdrop. One could almost imagine this was a stage setting for a play that was about to begin. For the people who lived on these boats, it was the play of everyday life that had been handed down from generation to generation. Across the street from this tranquil scenery, a large and modern shopping mall towered over an old, traditional marketplace next to it.

In a blink of an eye, one could go from the modern to the ancient, and we explored both. In the mall, again we saw stores with familiar names just like at home. However, it was the huge local market next to it that held our attention the longest. The smell of food cooking made me feel hungry, but not enough to eat. Some fruits and vegetables were unknown to us, in odd shapes and different colours, and we wondered how they should be prepared. The crafts, the racks upon racks of kimonos and traditional dresses, the artists displaying their paintings on rice paper or silk, and the fine needlepoint caught our interest. I debated for some time, asking the girls' opinions on which needlepoint to buy, finally settling on the one of two Vietnamese ladies in traditional dress who were balancing flower pots at each end of a pole which lay across their shoulders.

The sun was shining, and it was a perfect day, so when Ms. Le and Trevor showed up, we joined them at one of their special spots for—guess what? —yes, a bowl of Pho!

CHAPTER 15

The next morning when Trevor dropped us off at the dock, the sky was cloudy and the air felt cool and crisp. Danielle, Natalie, and I boarded a small cruise ship for a three-day, two-night cruise on Ha Long Bay.

"Sorry I can't be with you on this cruise. I wanted to join you but I need to get that kitchen finished and move into the apartment so we can spend more time together later this week. I will be right here waiting for you when you arrive."

"I am disappointed, too, but you can only be in one place at a time. I have been looking forward to doing this cruise, and I will enjoy it with the girls. I just hope it gets a little warmer."

The ship was small and cozy, only twenty-eight cabins. As we boarded we noticed only two other passengers were westerners. The dining room, being the largest area, had floor-to-ceiling windows casting light and shadow on the rich-looking hardwood tables, chairs, and walls. In the centre of the room stood several columns surrounded by serving tables. An impressive scale-size model of our boat was displayed next to one of the columns.

Soon after being welcomed with a tasty fruit drink and given the necessary safety instructions and a description of the ship's amenities, we explored the remainder of the ship. First, we checked our adjoining cabins. They were small but comfortable, with large sliding doors which opened onto a French balcony. On the deck, I was impressed by the teak wood floors, railing and furnishings, but it was the seascape that took my breath away! As we drifted from shore, I felt serene as I gazed at the calm teal water and the fascinating shapes of the islands. My thoughts drifted to Trevor and then to Paul, my two sons, both absent. I wished they could have been with us and wondered if it would ever happen. *Would we all be together at the same time in the same place?*

On the deck, our host and tour guide soon gathered the passengers to provide a brief summary of our schedule for the cruise. Each morning, a day boat would ferry us to interesting sites and islands in the bay. After the crowd dispersed, the host sat with Natalie, Danielle, and I for a while. He asked where we were from and spoke about learning English. It was becoming necessary, he said, considering all the tourists visiting the area. He also mentioned the caves that we would be visiting the next morning and suggested we might want to bring something to cover our heads.

"Why would we want to do that?" I asked, thinking he might be referring to the mornings being cool for a ride in a day boat.

"Because of the spiders," he retorted.

"Spiders! In the caves? I think I might not be interested in going to the caves," I said.

He laughed and walked away. *I have been in many caves in my travels*, I thought to myself, *and I have never had to cover my head in case of falling spiders. Or perhaps… I was just not told about the spiders?* Shivers ran up my spine at the thought of it! I resolved that I would not go on that outing.

In the evening, I joined the girls in their cabin and found them sitting on the bed playing a card game. When we get together as a family, we still enjoy playing board games. When Paul is present, Monopoly usually comes out, and the competition can go on until the wee hours of the morning.

"Want to play, Mom?" Danielle asked.

"No, I will just sit here and enjoy watching you play. Too bad we didn't bring Monopoly."

"Yeah! And too bad Paul is not here."

"Isn't it amazing that we are here?" I said. "Who could have ever imagined that someday we would find ourselves doing a cruise on Ha Long Bay in Vietnam?"

"We have come a long way from our little house on Babineau Road," Natalie affirmed.

"Yes, we have."

I slipped into the past, picturing us in that small but dearly loved house my sister and I designed. It was two years after the separation from my husband, and the house in Dalhousie had finally sold. During the eighties when interest rates were very high, twelve percent on a mortgage was considered good and the rates were often even higher. The combination of losing money on the house because it was undersold, paying the lawyers and other expenses meant I cleared about ten thousand dollars. I was very aware that if I lived off this money it would be gone within a year. I also knew how difficult it was to find a place to rent with three children, especially while running a daycare in my home to make a living. Almost forty years ago, I lived in a rented mobile home while babysitting six children and earning fifteen dollars a week for one child and twenty-five a week for a family of two. I felt trapped. I only had a high school education, so if I took a job, I would earn five dollars an hour and have to pay to have my children looked after. It was crucial that those ten thousand dollars be put to maximum use.

So, I took a chance. My sister and I drew a blueprint of a small house where everyone would have their own space. It looked like a doll's house. The main floor would have a kitchen, living room, bathroom, laundry room, and my bedroom. The finished basement had a bedroom for each child and a playroom for the them. Every room was tiny, and the whole house was thirty feet by twenty-four feet. When we brought the drawing to the architect, he laughed. We forgot to allow space for the walls, so the house had to be extended by two feet. I applied for loans in two different financial institutions, one of which loaned money, interest free, to needy families. However, neither one would agree to lend me the money until the other approved it. I bought a small parcel of land which I later paid for with a grant offered to home builders in order to stimulate the economy. I opened an account with a building supply store to buy materials. Since I could not afford to hire a contractor, I approached separate people to build. Someone to pour the foundation, a carpenter, a plumber, an electrician, and cabinet maker, offering them each a thousand dollars down and the remainder once the work was finished. We were so excited when construction began, but when the children and I would visit the construction site I would remind them not to get too attached to the house because it was not ours yet.

"Mommy may have to sell the lot with a basement on it." I'd explain.

Then my warning became that I would sell the lot with a frame and roof on it. Finally, I may have to sell the house because the loans had not yet been approved. After four months of waiting and making tiny payments at the supply store, I opened a letter that brought relief. The loans had been approved! We moved in two months later, on the same day Natalie started her first day of school.

My reminiscing was interrupted by Natalie's cough.

"What's going on?" I asked. "You have been coughing all evening."

"I don't know. My lungs are not feeling well. Probably from that bedroom in Cam Pha. Even if it was a non-smoking room, it really smelled like smoke."

We agreed to an early bedtime. Alone in my room I wrote a few words to Paul to let him know all was well, and I sent him photos.

The next morning at breakfast, we were given instructions about where to pick up our life jackets and board the day boat.

There were several small craft that carried twenty to thirty passengers each. Our first stop for sight-seeing was Ti Top Island, which was popular because of its clear water beach, soft white sand and climbing. On the climb, while dodging numerous tree branches and shrubs, I stopped several times to soak in the scenery and catch my breath. Layers of mountain peaks towered over the bay giving the impression that the dozens of large and small boats floating below were just toys. After climbing three-quarters of the way, I was happy to return to the beach and enjoy the milk from a freshly cut coconut. The girls made it all the way to the top after climbing more than four hundred steps. The view and the prized photos they captured was their reward.

Even though I knew day two included a visit to a cave, I followed the crowd. I had decided to go to the island, but I would just not enter Me Cung Cave. Surprise! Surprise! As we got to it, I was told I could not wait for the group at the entrance because they would be exiting in another direction. So up went my hood and in I went! It was not as traumatic as I had imagined. I do not have a great fear of spiders but I do not enjoy the thought of one falling on my head nor anywhere else on my body. I did not see a single spider, so I never found out whether the guide was joking or serious.

We then made a stop at the only pearl farm in Ha Long Bay for a demonstration of how pearls are grown and harvested. Next, we visited Cua Van Fishing Village, which has an intriguing story. We saw how families lived on floating houses for thousands of years. In 2014, the government ordered all these families to be moved inland in order to improve living facilities. Before 2014, this had been the largest of seven villages. People no longer live there, but they still fish and engage in other cultural activities. A portion of the village is now being kept as a museum. A woman wearing the now-familiar conical hat took great pride in explaining the traditions and culture of the past communities.

"Children," she said, "would learn to swim before they reached the age of four."

She escorted us to the old classroom which served as the school for primary and intermediate students.

"Now they go to school inland," she explained with a sigh. She talked about the living customs and honouring ancestors, and how so much had changed.

"Some good, some losses," she said.

I was moved as she described how these people had lived off the sea, free from the pressures of modern society for so long. Now their income is mostly from tourism. Many earn a living by filling their small boats with fresh water, potato chips, handmade toys, pearls, and even some clothing and selling to tourists on the small cruise ships. Passengers who answer their call by opening the French patio doors receive their purchased items from net baskets at the end of a long pole.

When we woke up the following morning, it was evident that Natalie's cough had gotten worse. The air was chilly, and the prospect of going to a damp cave did not seem like a good idea, so she decided it was wise not to go. As for me, when I read the description of the trek through the cave, I worried that there would be too much climbing. Yes, perhaps the thought of the possible spiders influenced me a little. I chose to stay behind, visit the gift shop, and enjoy the sun deck. Danielle did not want to miss the adventure, so off she went. Upon her return we were delighted to share parts of her experience through photos of the large and beautiful Hang Sung Sot Cave along with some of the amazing sights of the day.

The next morning our cruise ended. It had been another memorable experience to cherish. Trevor met us at the dock and took us to our hotel in Ha Long where we would be staying for the next few days. He would return to work and pick us up in a few hours.

CHAPTER 16

As I unpacked my suitcase and placed my cosmetic bag on the bathroom counter of our new hotel room, I heard one of the girls ask, "So, what's the plan for the rest of the day?" I did not pay much attention to the answer. I was thinking of Trevor and how the question of generations was important to him. When he had searched for me, his motivation was to know about his bloodline; anything else would be a bonus. He wanted to know where he came from, who his ancestors were, what they did and where they had lived, which was understandable. By being immersed in family stories, growing up with relatives, and developing behaviour patterns, my children had already learned this little by little. Our family had become somewhat predictable. Usually, the response to a simple question such as, "What's the plan for the remainder of the day?" would have been answered by the traditional, "I don't know, what would you like to do?" Brainstorming the available options would follow, and we usually reached consensus on an activity. Trevor, on the other hand, knew nothing about our typical behaviour patterns and we knew nothing of his, so there was always an element of surprise.

When he showed up at the hotel, for example, he asked if we would be interested in visiting Sun World Park, the one we had spotted on the first day of our arrival in Ha Long. I had been so fascinated by the huge Ferris wheel that I had squealed with excitement, "Wow! I would love to go on that wheel!" It reminded me of the Big Eye in London, England. I had always regretted not riding it when I had visited the city.

"We could ride the cable car to Mystic Mountain and go for a ride on the big wheel," he suggested.

"Are you serious?" I asked.

"Of course! Why, have you changed your mind?"

"No, I would love to go. I just can't believe you're actually going to take us there. It has been years since anyone took me to an amusement park!"

He glanced at the girls, and before he could even ask the question, they answered in unison, "No thanks!" They would come to the park, but it was clear neither one had any desire to get on the wheel. The girls' preference would be to visit the lower section of the park, which looked amazing with its ornate arches, castles, and animal-shaped flower displays. The four of us would meet up later.

As the cable car lifted us up over the water, the panoramic view took my breath away. Suspended in the air we could observe the boat traffic travelling up and down the bay, circling hundreds of islands. We could see the crowded city in the distance and even spot our hotel. I didn't mind that the cable car was crowded. Trevor explained the cabin could hold two hundred passengers, making it the biggest cable cabin in the world.

"Well, now I have been in the largest cable cabin in Asia. When I visited Switzerland several years back, I travelled in Europe's highest cable car. It took us to the top of Klein Matterhorn, known as the Little Matterhorn, where we walked on glaciers."

"You have travelled a lot."

"I agree, however, that was only in the last eighteen years. Before that, it was much more of a struggle."

"I want to hear all about it and all about your life."

After we disembarked, we walked a short distance to the edge of the mountain and stood by a fence looking down over the cliff. I do not remember the view or how high up we were, nor do I remember feeling afraid of the height; I was focused on hearing all about his life. We took the plunge and began to share intimate information about our lives. He questioned my journey, where I had lived, when I got married, and how long since my divorce. He asked about his bloodline—his grandfathers and grandmothers, my immediate family and other family members. He was interested in learning about the other men in the family— who were they and what did they stand for? I was proud to say I was very fond of them and explained that, just like him, many had started their own businesses.

I heard about his childhood illnesses and his work experiences as a young adult. Little by little, I learned about his mom and how she died in a car accident.

"My mother always believed I would find you some day because she knew how much I wanted to. I have wanted to meet you all my life. When I was younger, I tried several times. From social services, I eventually learned you had another son and that you were married and lived in northern New Brunswick. I was maybe twenty-four at the time. I lived in Ottawa, which was about one thousand kilometres away. I remember getting in my little Datsun and driving to Campbellton, New Brunswick. I planned to go there and search for you, to knock on every door if it was necessary. I went to all the schools in the area, spoke to the principals, and searched the yearbooks but found nothing. I guess it just wasn't the right time."

"It probably was not," I answered. Our eyes met and my mind darted back to where my life would have been at the time. "I don't know how I would have reacted back then."

We were silent for a few moments, reliving in our minds the circumstances of our lives, when Trevor's phone rang. Ms. Le was on the other end, and it was heartwarming to hear him say, with a smile on his face, "I am standing on Mystic Mountain talking with my mother."

After he hung up, we returned to our conversation. He shared his vision for the future of the learning centres.

"I will retire in Canada someday," he said. "But now, let's go! We have to get to that big wheel you're so excited about."

There was a spectacular 360° view of Ha Long Bay from the top of the big wheel. However, the experience was not half as exciting as it had been in my younger years when we would ride on the Ferris wheel in Shediac. We would sit in a box-like seat in the open air. There were no seat belts, only a metal bar which was drawn down in front of us to keep us from falling out. Yet we challenged one another to rock the seats and sometimes even leaned over backwards to see our friends above or below us. We had no fears; we lived in the excitement of the moment and believed nothing could harm us. Our hearts would rise and fall as we ascended the highest point, and we could hardly catch our breath from laughing.

Being on the big wheel with Trevor was very different. Each unit was a cabin, so there were no rocking seats. We entered through a door, and benches were positioned around the walls. We chose to stand. There was no fresh air, but we were surrounded by windows which did permit us to enjoy the view. Other than the excitement of being there with Trevor, it was a pretty calm ride.

"Want a few photos?" Trevor asked as he pulled out his phone and held it up so we could take a selfie.

"Sure, I would love a photo of the two of us suspended here in mid-air. This is nice but not as exciting as when we were young. Remember the Bill Lynch Show in Shediac during Lobster Festival?"

Trevor remembered. "Isn't it amazing that all of us—you, your three children and I—grew up in the same area?"

"Yes, it's very strange. As we talk about our childhood, we all have pictures in our minds that are similar."

The big wheel stopped and we stepped out. The air was getting cooler. We stood below the wheel, gazing up at the height of it. Trevor lit a cigarette.

"Would you care for hot chocolate?" he asked.

"I would love a hot chocolate."

Once we had settled at a table away from most of the other clientele, we continued talking about Shediac.

"Do you remember Parlee Beach?" I asked.

Parlee Beach is one of the most beautiful sandy beaches in the Maritime Provinces. The water is warm, and it's perfect for a swim. It had been an important part of my teen years. In the summer, we would look forward to the American tourists arriving. They wore white shorts and T-shirts and looked rich. There was a building on the beach which was built on stilts. It was a place where we could dance to rock and roll music from the jukebox with the new guys who came from the USA. That made them important in our eyes.

Trevor laughed. He also had been to Parlee Beach, but the jukebox was no longer there.

"However," he shared, "most of the time my friends and I preferred to jump off the one-lane bridge in Grande-Digue. Many times, the police would come and chase us away, but we always went back."

"Oh my gosh, Trevor! That was extremely dangerous. I remember seeing children doing that, and I was so glad it was not one of my sons jumping off that bridge. You mean to tell me all along it *was* one of mine!"

That evening as we walked through the park, I savoured every moment. I was with my son at an amusement park, and he with his mom. It was clear that we wanted to spend more time together on Mystic Mountain. We decided to let the girls know that he would be taking me out for dinner and they could go on without us. We stood in line for a long time trying to get onboard a small train-like go-cart that toured the park, then continued our exploration on foot until darkness began to fall. We discovered a pristine Zen Garden where the sand had been raked in harmonious circles around the carefully placed rocks, so we sat for a while and listened to the trickling water sounds of the fountain. It was calming and peaceful.

Several hours passed quickly, and when we started to make our way back towards the exit of the park, we again passed near the now empty coffee shop.

"Time for another hot chocolate?" Trevor asked.

I found a cozy corner for us to sit and relax while he ordered. He was quiet as he placed the two cups on the table. He seemed pensive. Sitting across from me, Trevor took my hands and asked, "Are you ready now to talk about it?"

I slowly nodded.

"I need to know," he said. "I need to know what happened and who my father is."

"It happened late one night," I began. "I had found a job and he was my shift supervisor. I do not know the man or remember what he looks like. I had only been working there for four, maybe five nights. That evening, four of us girls had worked late. I don't remember if the subway was shut down for the night or if our supervisor thought it was too late for us to take it. He called for a taxi and waited outside with us. When the cab arrived, the taxi driver was not kind. He was upset because the other girls were to be driven to one end of the city while I was to be driven in the other direction. He finally agreed to take all of us, but in a harsh tone he said he would drop off the others and then take care of me. I was scared and not feeling comfortable about getting in with him, so I asked my supervisor to call another cab for me. He said he would take me home. Then he pointed to an apartment building close by, saying that it was where he lived. We could walk over and get his car, and then he would drive me. As we approached the building he pointed to a window where the light was on and said his friends were probably still up. We would go get the car keys and then be off. When we walked into his apartment it was empty, which was when I knew I was in trouble. I was raped that night."

Fear welled up inside of me as I spoke. There was a trembling in my belly and a tightness in my jaw. My heart was pounding, and I recognized the old fear imprinted in my body.

Breathe, I told myself. *Just breathe.*

Although I was in touch with the fear, I noticed I felt safe with Trevor. I focused on the warmth of his strong hands holding mine. It was soothing, and I felt comforted by his presence. It was Trevor who broke the silence as he pulled his hands from mine.

"I want to find him. I want to look that man in the eye."

"No, please. Please don't look for him. I am still afraid of him. I have been afraid all my life that he would find me. He did my interview; he had all my personal information, and he knew where I was from. He warned me never to tell anyone. If I did, he would find me. He doesn't know you exist. I left the city a few days after, but I have always been afraid."

"It should be the other way around," Trevor said. "He should be afraid of you. You can prove it now with DNA."

That was true. It took a few moments before I could reply.

"I honestly do not want to go there again. I don't have the courage nor the strength. I do not want to do that. Please, wait until I die, then you can look for him if you want to."

Again, there was a long silence. As I looked into Trevor's eyes, I saw kindness and understanding, which I took as a sign that he would do nothing for now, but I did not verify if my perception was true. The silence felt long, though in reality it lasted only a few short seconds.

"Let's go for a walk." he suggested.

We walked through the amusement park, which was quiet in that section. The quietness felt heavy.

"May I take your hand?" he asked softly.

I looked up to him, smiled and slipped my hand into his. It felt as if he was just a little boy walking in an amusement park holding his mommy's hand. I was so happy to be walking in that park with my little six-foot son.

As we walked, I felt my thoughts shift. I realized that I had no more reason to fear the man who raped me, so I shared that thought with Trevor.

"He is probably an old man by now," I said, feeling brave. "And if he ever showed up, I could push him down the stairs!"

We both chuckled a little.

The path we were on led us to the Zen garden. We sat there for some time, side-by-side, in silence. Something within me had changed. I was able to let go of the fear of the old man. That fear was only alive in my mind because I kept it there. I had just met the son of the man who had raped me. And I loved him. I was his mother. I needed to embrace the whole story. I found within me the young lady who had been raped, the twice "unwed mother of the sixties" who had been shamed because a new life was growing within her.

I love you, I said to her in silence. *You are amazing, and you have two amazing sons.*

Mystic Mountain was truly symbolic because what happened there felt like a mystical experience.

CHAPTER 17

Co To Island

We had only a few days left of our visit. While planning our trip Trevor had asked if there was something in particular which we would like to see, so we let him know we preferred nature to city. We loved beaches and walking trails.

Trevor wanted to treat us to a wonderful island resort, and he said Co To Island was relaxing and quiet with beautiful beaches and cliffs. It also boasted friendly people and beautiful, modern hotels and restaurants. He had booked our last few days and planned to travel with the three of us and his girlfriend to this paradise island. It was the farthest inhabited island from the mainland, and very few foreigners visited.

We planned to eat at his restaurant before boarding the boat in Van Don, which was a thirty-minute drive away. We were sitting in the restaurant and had already ordered our meals when Trevor decided to check the time of the last boat to leave mid-afternoon. It had been cancelled, and the last boat would be leaving in approximately half an hour! Our meals became takeout! Trevor quickly went into the kitchen to grab a few baguettes, some ham and cheese to take along just in case we might be hungry at odd times. We all piled into the car. The driver made good time, honking his horn all the way to let the parade of traffic know we were in a hurry.

At the dock, passports were required and questions were asked.

"Why are you going to Co To Island?"

Adrenaline ran high as we watched the boat prepare to leave. Finally, we got the okay to board. We walked the plank and entered the boat. Attendants grabbed our suitcases, piled them in the front cabin next to the captain, and we were off. Relieved that we had made it in time, we settled in the few seats that remained and enjoyed our meal.

An hour and a half by jetboat, and away from the crowds, we saw that the island had the potential to live up to its reputation. However, when we reached it, disembarking proved to be a challenge. The tide was low, so the boat happened to be three feet below the wharf without stairs or a ladder to climb. As we exited carrying our suitcases, we were instructed to walk along the ledge, which was no more than a foot wide, to the front of the boat. We handed our suitcases to a few men who then lifted, pulled, and yanked us out of the boat and onto the wharf. Some of the younger people managed to climb out with just a helping hand. However, it took two men, one on the left and one on the right, to hoist me up as my feet scrambled on the side of the dock to make it to the top. It was like walking up a wall!

From the wharf, we were taken by golf cart to our hotel. The building was so new that there was still some construction going on. We checked in, were given keys to our rooms on the fifth floor and advised that there was no restaurant in the hotel. Strangely, there seemed to be no one else around. Anxious to explore our surroundings, the five of us walked to the street closest to the water where many new hotels had been built. We were confident that we would find a nice restaurant for dinner. We found vendors lining the street selling meat, fish, and a few handmade items, several of them signalling us with a wave of the hand to pick a fish, a squid, or other type of sea creature from their large water-filled tubs. I understood that they would be happy to cook for us, and I am certain we missed out on a special experience of dining with a local family and tasting delicacies of the sea. However, since being ill during my visit to China, I was less adventurous when it came to street vendors. It may have been my loss, but it was also my choice! Smiles and questioning nods were frequent as we strolled by these friendly and curious residents.

We were on a mission to find a hotel with a restaurant or at least a nice place to eat, and we walked to the very end of the hotel-lined street. To our great surprise we found out that all but one hotel—the one in which we were the only guests—were closed. All the restaurants were also closed because it was not tourist season! We chose to laugh at the situation and consoled ourselves by taking a long walk on the beach. It was a beautiful afternoon. The beach was deserted except for the five of us. The sun was warm on our faces, and the sound of the waves gently faded as they reached the sandy beach. In spite of the fact that we were on a faraway island, the surroundings felt similar to so many of the beaches back home.

As we strolled together mostly silent and alone in our own thoughts, I thought of my dad. Perhaps it was the serenity of the moment or the distance from the rest of the world that made me feel nostalgic. Perhaps it was a moment of simply being, a pure moment uncontaminated by obligations, expectations, or judgements. Or perhaps it was the presence of the redhead walking behind me that brought the image of my dad's smiling face to mind. Whatever it was, I felt at peace. There was a moment of acceptance. Being with Trevor brought a feeling of the presence of my father. No need to analyse, explain, or deny. He is not my father, but he is *of* my father. He carries his genes, as do my other three children. He has a greater resemblance to him, and he brings back a clearer memory of him. I gave myself permission to savour the joy it brought to me.

Walking back to the hotel on another street, we found a general store where we could buy water, noodles, crackers, tea, and ice cream. Word quickly got around that there were foreigners on the island, so residents turned to take a second look as we walked by and children came to the window to see us. Occasionally, a door would open, and giggling children waved and shouted.

"Hello, hello, hello, hello!"

One little boy was so taken by one of my daughters that he tripped over his own feet while looking up at her as he went by. We refrained from laughing so as not to cause him embarrassment. It was a precious moment.

When we arrived at the hotel, the lady at the desk offered to lend us the golf cart to check out a restaurant that might be open farther down on the island. The girls and I decided to settle in our rooms, and Trevor's baguettes and cheese were very much appreciated. He and his girlfriend borrowed the owner's motorbike and went off searching for this other restaurant that apparently had wonderful seafood. They didn't have any luck, so they returned to share the ham and cheese.

Beds in Vietnam tend to be very firm, and it was difficult to get to sleep. The wind came up and howled all night. It was cold, and it took a while for me to figure out the heating system, so I only managed to sleep for a few hours. The girls were down the hall just a few rooms away, and they had the food and the tea! I did not want to wake them up early in the morning, so I thought I would send a message on my iPad asking them to let me know when they were awake. To my surprise there was already a message from Danielle: "Mom, the kettle is on for your tea!"

They had not slept much either. Natalie was not feeling well at all, and the cough was getting worse. She was sitting in bed, under the blankets, wearing several sweatshirts, a scarf wrapped around her neck, and a tuque on her head. Danielle also woke up with a cough and a slight fever. I was worried, so I walked down the hall to Trevor's room and knocked on the door.

"Can we go home, please?" I said, as he opened the door.

I saw the bewildered look in his eyes. "What home?" he asked.

"Well, not *home* home. Back to your place. This isn't working out. We couldn't sleep last night. Natalie is sick and now Danielle is also coughing and feverish."

"Sure, give me a few minutes and we'll go to the ticket office at the wharf and get tickets for the first boat out."

The girls and I had a small breakfast as we waited to see what time we would be leaving. Soon Trevor was back.

"We have the tickets, but the boat won't be leaving this morning because of strong winds. Perhaps after lunch, around one o'clock, if the winds die down."

Trevor and I decided to take a walk and search for a coffee shop. We had seen signs the previous day, but none of the shops were open. We did spot a house which seemed to have an open area with a few tables. A lady pulled out a chair and kindly invited us to have a seat. Trevor managed to make her understand that we were looking for a coffee-house, and she immediately heated some water and offered us a cup. Besides the fact that I am not a coffee drinker, the coffee looked very strong and thick. Molasses was what came to my mind. I certainly meant no offence by saying, "No, thank you."

Trevor politely drank some while I amused myself with the woman's little daughter, who seemed not much older than a year. She was adorable and not at all put out by two strangers sitting in their house. She walked up to me, put her two little arms up and let me help her onto the chair next to me. The mother offered her two playing cards—a seven of spades and a five of diamonds—to keep her entertained. We spent a very pleasant half hour playing with the baby and enjoying this welcome and novel environment.

As noon approached, our suitcases were ready and we checked out of the hotel. We waited for the golf cart to take us to the wharf. The attendant at the desk called the ticket office only to find out that the boat would not leave at one o'clock. Perhaps one would leave around three. She was informed that someone from the ticket office would call the hotel to notify the foreigners when the boat was ready to leave. As three o'clock drew near and we had received no calls yet, Trevor and I walked to the wharf to see if we could get more information. The ticket office was closed, and a handful of people were waiting. Fishing boats were lined on the left side of the wharf. I stopped in amazement to examine these boats made of bamboo. Trevor had told me they were out fishing that morning on the rough water. We wondered how these little boats could survive in the wind while our jetboat, which was tied to two posts on the right side of the wharf, couldn't make the crossing. A short man with a black attaché case noticed we were speaking English and advised us that there would be no boat leaving today. Trevor was not impressed. He was frustrated. We returned to the hotel, checked in again, and decided to make the best of it.

Despite the wind, it was a beautiful sunny day, so back to the beach we went. In the distance, the waters may have been turbulent but not so on the beach. A serene landscape lay in front of us: seashells, seaweed, an abandoned fishing boat still anchored on the beach, and our footprints in the wet sand. Without phones, gadgets, and the hustle and bustle of ordinary life, simple things stood out, as did extraordinary things! Danielle showed us small holes in the sand surrounded by tiny, perfectly rounded balls of sand. She explained that these little pellets were made by a species of crustacean that is found in the tropics. They live in burrows in the sand and are called sand bubbler crabs.

On the way back to the hotel, we visited a small shrine and explored more of the community. We made another stop at the general store, then settled into the girls' room for the evening. I enjoyed hearing Trevor and the girls compare notes about growing up in the same area without knowing about each other; they had a few things in common. They had sat in the same school bus and travelled the same route. They remembered the bus drivers and some of the teachers. They brought up the names of friends and laughed at some of their school experiences. Danielle shared some photos she had copied from the old school albums. It was surreal, and yet sometimes sad for me, to see pictures of school teams that included both my sons. Trevor and Paul, two brothers who were often on the same teams, their photos sometimes close together on the same page.

In the morning, the wind had died down, and we had slept better. Natalie was still not feeling well, but the fever seemed to have broken. Danielle's cough, however, was getting worse. We were up early, suitcases packed and ready to catch the eight o'clock boat. Again, we were told that the sea was too rough and perhaps it would leave in the afternoon. It was Sunday morning. By now, we were feeling anxious about missing our return flight home from Hanoi early Monday morning. Danielle was especially worried since she had to be back at work in a few days. Trevor was becoming very annoyed at the service and suspecting that perhaps the boat was not leaving because there were too few passengers to make the crossing, so he offered to hire a chartered boat. He was certain that some of the fisherman would take us across. It would be a four-hour crossing on a fishing boat.

"No way!" I exclaimed. "There is no way I will do the crossing in a bamboo boat! I would be terrified!"

Danielle wrote to her employer asking to find a tentative replacement in case we missed our flight. Around one o'clock in the afternoon, the woman at the front desk received a call asking her to advise us that the boat was leaving at one thirty. In no time at all, we were at the wharf boarding the jetboat. It was a rough ride, but we were so happy to be on board.

Once on the mainland, a driver was waiting to pick us up. We made a quick stop at Trevor's restaurant to pick up some food to eat on the way. We still had a four-hour drive to Hanoi, and it would soon be dark. I told Trevor there was no point in him accompanying us to Hanoi since we were leaving very early in the morning, which made it difficult and awkward to say our goodbyes and thank yous because we were so rushed. Trevor apologised profusely about our experience on Co To Island.

"Please, don't feel bad about that trip. Your intention was good, and you had no way of knowing how it would turn out. Besides, how many people get to visit Co To Island? It was an adventure. I am happy to have lived it, and it will be a great story to tell our friends back home."

We hugged and promised to see one another again in two years at the latest. Ms. Le was there to wish us well and express hope that we would come again. Trevor hugged the girls and thanked them for coming all the way to Vietnam. Then he hugged me again.

"I promise that in two years we will do a cruise together, and it will be great. I have always wanted to visit Italy."

I acknowledged with a nod. Looking into his eyes I recognized this to be our second goodbye. A memory of a baby being wheeled out of the delivery room darted across my mind. For an instant, I felt a blanket of regrets begin to cover me. I regretted not being happy when I carried him. I regretted not holding him at birth and not being there for him to guide his path as he grew up. But it was just a flash. I gave myself permission to have regrets for a moment, then I remembered to treat myself with kindness. I let my heart be filled with gratitude, and this time I said in silence, *Thank you, God, for looking after him. We are going to be all right.* I gave him one last hug and one last smile, knowing I would see him again someday. There were no tears, just a heavy yet grateful heart.

By the time we arrived in Hanoi, Danielle was not at all well. At the hotel, Natalie and I went to get a bite to eat and Danielle went to bed. Again, I grew worried. We were flying by way of Hong Kong, and the last time we had been through that airport there were body temperature scans. What if she had a fever and was unable to board the plane?

The night was short as we had to rise early for the flight, but it felt very long. Many scenarios ran through my mind. Danielle was barely awake when she popped the thermometer in her mouth. Natalie and I waited.

"No fever!" she exclaimed.

I breathed a sigh of relief!

Before leaving the room, I sent one last thank you message to Trevor.

Hi Dear,

Wanted to say thank you so much for the wonderful time together. Thanks for everything… even Co To Island! Have no regrets!

I will always remember our first afternoon together and our time at the amusement park. Those were my favourite and special times. Thank you for showing up in my life. You are a great gift.

I love you,
Yolande

We grabbed our belongings and met the driver. I settled the bill at the front desk, and as we were about to exit the hotel, I heard a ding on my iPad. There was a message from Trevor. Knowing there would be no Wi-Fi in the cab, I opened it quickly and downloaded it so I would be able to read it en route to the airport.

Long-lost Mother…

You did the right thing that day on April 20, 1970. We would have never understood each other, and I know that is the truth. We both have had hard roads and we are better for it. I could not have imagined a happier, more insightful, spirited, and loving woman than the one I was with on Mystic Mountain. It was an incredible day, and I will cherish it until the day I die. You were more than I could have ever expected from a woman who has been through so much. You are amazing and great. This was the right time to meet, not five or ten years ago, nor five or ten years from now. This was the time. We will take a cruise someday, and it will be awesome! I cannot wait for it. Until you get home, sleep as much as possible, and, when you close your eyes, remember that I love you and am grateful that you came here into my life.

Bonne nuit!
Jean-Marc (the name I had given him at birth)

EPILOGUE

R eflections... returning home, I felt happy and content. I had met my son and felt the story of Trevor and I finding each other was complete. Now we would live out the relationship as it unfolded, mostly by communicating through video chat and visiting when the opportunity arose. It had become a reality.

Three years later, I find myself sitting comfortably on my sofa, remembering the day I received the letter from the social worker. Again, I look outside at the green grass and the leaves shimmering in the breeze and realize how much has changed. They look the very same as the day I received that first letter, but they are not the same. Just as I appear to be the same person, but I am changed.

The hiding and the silence began long ago as a way of protecting myself from the harsh judgement of being an "unwed mother" in the sixties. To protect my sanity I stored all the events in a box in my mind and in my heart and, with great discipline, never dwelled on them. I did not know at that time that this was trauma. I did not know how I would survive. I just knew I had to put things behind me and keep going. I was desperate. Over the years, counselling helped, but what I felt truly saved my life was getting involved in personal growth and self-healing. I wanted to learn how to be happy, and I was motivated to take care of myself so that I could better take care of my children. I wanted them to be happy. I longed to heal the hurts that had been lodged in my heart since the death of my dad, so I read many self-help books, I attended sessions on personal and spiritual growth, and I learned to ask for help.

Healing is a process, and awareness is the key. Once I grew more attuned to the conversations in my head and got to know myself as the child who had lost her dad and the young adult who became pregnant, I discovered how to help myself. This did not happen overnight. Gradually, I discovered that I was not just a victim, and I had the power to let go of the old stories and create new ones.

On the morning I received the letter from the social worker telling me my son was searching for me, I thought I was going to die. The good life I had created for myself, behind the wall of protection, was in jeopardy. The secret was out, and people would judge and reject me again. I was scared! In trying to hold myself together, I had scribbled these few words in my journal: "I have travelled to many countries in the world, but I am about to embark on an adventure like no other. One which only I can take, for it is my story. It is a journey straight into my heart." I needed to make a choice: hold on to the old story or begin a new one. The image of the baby left behind in the delivery room was vivid in my mind and heart—it was the only memory I had of him. And again, I was motivated by wanting to do better—to be better for the child I had given up and for the ones I kept. I am convinced that as we heal, something in our children heals also, even when they are adults.

Things have changed deep inside me. There is a lightness and a freedom about just being me. I no longer have to hide, even from myself. I can just be. I catch myself reflecting on what has changed, and I discover that the shame is gone and has been replaced by gratitude. The fear is gone, replaced by peace. The hurt is gone, replaced by joy. I am still getting used to saying that I have four children when asked. And sometimes, when I don't feel secure enough or I think it will turn into a long story, I catch myself saying, "Three—I have three children." Then in my heart I say, *Sorry, Trevor, I love you and I am getting better at just saying the truth without excuses and justification.* Sometimes I say, "Four—I have four children," and I am proud.

I am conscious and grateful that some of the choices Trevor made contributed to the relationship we enjoy today. First, and most helpful to me, was the fact that he used an agency to find me. Being contacted first by a third person permitted me to prepare myself, as much as possible, for the first contact with him. It showed respect for me and the present circumstances of my life. Had he chosen to simply show up, I do not know what my reaction would have been. He may have been rejected again through no fault of his own, or mine. Giving me the opportunity to prepare was a gift. Going slowly built trust and a feeling of safety; he gave me the time and freedom to make a choice. He wanted me to have a second chance to let him into my life. Little did he know that one of his greatest gifts was his search for truth. His motto, Nothing but the truth, was an invitation for me to seek even more truth in my own life.

So why did I write this book? When I returned home after my trip to Vietnam to meet Trevor, I received an advisory note from the Department of Social Development in New Brunswick. It explained that as of April 2018 all adoption records which had been kept sealed for almost one hundred years would be opened. Adult adoptees and birth parents would now be able to access the information. My heart went out to all the long-lost moms still in hiding, wondering if they, too, still felt the pain and shame of the past. I wondered about all the long-lost sons and daughters who were searching and wanting to know the truth. I also thought about the great number of adoptive parents who might worry how this would affect their lives.

For a moment, I was in touch with the great pain and the fear which I thought would be felt by many, as they would have new challenges to face. And from the bottom of my heart, I felt a calling: *You have to write a book.* The answer? A strong *Yes.* I knew I needed to share our story, and so a new journey began. Trevor gave me permission and even allowed me to include our correspondence. Next, I had to learn how to write a book because I had never done this before. Then the writing began.

My intention in writing this book is to inspire hope, diminish fear, and encourage others to face their past and make peace with it. It is in no way advising parent or child to search or not to search—to answer the call or not—or to enter into a relationship or remain distant. I share my story in the hope that others will face their own story, challenge their thoughts, name their fears, and explore their options. Then they can make the courageous choices which are appropriate and healthy for them according to their own lives, values, and circumstances.

Writing *Long-Lost Mom* has been life-giving, fulfilling, and healing. I am so grateful to have said yes to living the experience.

Trevor did keep his promise. As the two-year anniversary of our first reunion approached, he contacted me to discuss the possibility of going on a cruise together. After researching the options, we both agreed that perhaps the money would be better spent if he came home to Canada for a visit. Next summer is a possibility.

ACKNOWLEDGMENTS

My heart is overflowing with gratitude for all those who have supported me in bringing this book to fruition.

To my son Trevor, for having the courage to seek and find me. For giving me the freedom to express my side of our story as I lived it and the strength to help me face and heal my past. This book would not be without you.

To Natalie, my daughter and loyal sounding board, who listened as I made sense of it all, edited before the editors, solved technical issues, and helped with page layout. Thank you, Natalie, for all your time, knowledge, love, and support.

To my son Paul and daughter Danielle, who encouraged me to be faithful to my calling and write the book. Your support, kindness, and love gave me the courage and determination to do it even though I was afraid.

To Trevor Corkum, my writing coach, who inspired me and kept me on track by showing me how to fully develop my ideas. Your gentle approach pushed me to go deeper into the story and reveal even more of myself. You have become more than a coach; you are a friend. Thank you for your many extra hours.

To the members of Icedash, my hometown writing group, who welcomed me as a first-time book author almost five years ago. You encouraged me, listened to my readings, gave me feedback to improve my writing, and inspired me with your writings. A special thank you to Warren Redman and Sarah Johnston for the extra editing and coaching.

To my numerous friends and family members, who lent an ear as I spent hours talking about my book throughout this process. Your time, attention, understanding, and encouragement are precious to me. This also applies to my website subscribers who have sent supportive messages after reading my blog posts. I hold all of you in my heart with gratitude.

My sincere gratitude also, to those who have provided very considerate endorsements.

To all of you who are reading this book, Thank you!

Made in United States
Orlando, FL
19 February 2023

30134392R00114